# The Guide

GW00836533

The Guide was originally produced by the Peddars Wa
inaugural meeting in Swaffham on 14th November
objectives:-

1.  To press for official designation and completi
2.  To promote and publicise the use of the route and its amenities for the benefit of walkers and cyclists.
3.  To promote a body of informed opinion that will improve the enjoyment and knowledge of Peddars Way.

As these original objectives appeared to have been achieved and maintenance of the Guide and Accommodation list seemed to be the remaining work, the Peddars Way Association was wound-up at a meeting of members at Dereham on 23rd March 1996, it was agreed that all the assets of the Association should be transferred to the Norfolk Area of the Ramblers' Association, which would continue to edit, publish and distribute the guide book.

The guide is intended to help you plan a holiday or just a day's walk on part of the track and has been kept as simple and inexpensive as possible. The route is described by means of twelve maps, the first seven of which should be read from bottom to top, and the last five from top to bottom. The maps are not fully to scale, but an indication of distance is shown on each sheet. Additional text is there to help you through the trickier sections. There is a separate list to help with accommodation, public transport and places of interest.

If you discover anything needing correction or additional information that would improve the guide, we would like to hear from you, the Guide Editors' addresses are below.

The Ordnance Survey Landranger maps (1:50,000) numbers 144, 132, 133 and 134 are recommended for the extra detail and information they contain. Even more detail is in the Explorer maps (1:25000) 229, 236, 250, 251, 252 and OL 40.

**GUIDE
EDITORS**

Sheila Smith, Caldcleugh, Old Buckenham,
Attleborough, Norfolk, NR17 1RU
Ian Mitchell
5, Montcalm Road, Norwich, NR1 4HX

Telephone 01603 622539

**DISTRIBUTION** Sheila Smith - address as above

## ACKNOWLEDGEMENTS:

Original maps and route descriptions by Alan & Penny Jenyon.
Ian Smith & Colin Hills.
Accommodation list by Sheila Smith, Ian Mitchell, John Kent & Derek Goddard
Computer layout by Sheila Smith.

Published by:  The Ramblers Association,  Norfolk Area

Copyright:  The Ramblers Association
39th Edition. Revised and reprinted regularly. February 2009

# Introduction

A guide to a route of 149 miles (239 kilometres), showing the surprising variety of Norfolk scenery from Knettishall Heath on the Suffolk border to Great Yarmouth.

The **PEDDARS WAY** is an ancient track, mainly Roman in the form in which we see today, but probably pre-Roman in origin. The original route may have run from Colchester to Lincolnshire, with a ferry or ford over the Wash. Peddars Way certainly contributed to the downfall of Queen Boadicea and the Iceni tribes. The surviving part of the route stretches from Knettishall Heath near Thetford in the south, to the coast at Holme. The Secretary of State for the Environment approved the Countryside Commission's proposals in Oct.1982 for a long distance route of 93 miles (149kms) to be known as **THE PEDDARS WAY and NORFOLK COAST PATH.**

**THE FOOTPATH WAS OFFICIALLY OPENED on JULY 8<sup>th</sup> 1986 by**

**HRH. PRINCE CHARLES.**

The **WEAVERS WAY** footpath, from Cromer to Gt. Yarmouth, devised by Norfolk County Council has been included in this guide as a continuation of the long distance path and adding another 56 miles (90kms).

A further route called the **ANGLES WAY** has been created by Norfolk & Suffolk County Councils, to link the Weavers Way at Yarmouth to the Peddars Way at Knettishall Heath, thus creating a circular route of 226 miles (362kms).

| TABLE OF DISTANCES | miles | kilometres |
|---|---|---|
| PEDDARS WAY | 47 | 75 |
| NORFOLK COAST PATH | 46 | 74 |
| Long Distance Path Total | 93 | 149 |
| WEAVERS WAY | 56 | 90 |
| Total covered in Guide | 149 | 239 |
| ANGLES WAY | 77 | 123 |
| Total "Round Norfolk" | 226 | 362 |

**ICENI WAY** - A walk from Knettishall Heath via Thetford & Brandon along the banks of the Little & Great Ouse to Kings Lynn and via Sandringham to Hunstanton. This includes a 15mile (24kms) off-road route between Knettishall Heath and Thetford. The Iceni Way and Peddars Way together can provide a 130 mile (210 km) circuit with easier transport links.

Guides & accommodation lists for the **Angles Way** and the **Iceni Way** are available from Ramblers Association, Sheila Smith, Caldcleugh, Cake Street, Old Buckenham, Attleborough, NR17 1RU. They each cost £3.10, including post and packing. Details of our other publications are available on request, or see www.norfolkra.org.uk

**A cloth badge**, to commemorate your journey along the
**Peddars Way & Norfolk Coast Path**, is available. For details contact: -
The National Trail Office, The Old Courthouse, Baron's Close, Fakenham, Norfolk, NR21 8BE
Email: nationaltrail@norfolk.gov.uk. Tel: 01328 850530
A **Weavers Way Badge** may be obtained from Norfolk County Council - ask for a
"Weavers' Way Challenge" card before you start the walk:-
T.01603 223317   or   Room 301, County Hall, Martineau Lane, Norwich, NR1 2SG

# Peddars Way & Norfolk Coast Path

## Symbols used on maps

| | | | |
|---|---|---|---|
| Major roads | Railway | Church | S Shop |
| Minor roads | Disused Railway | Windmill/windpump | PH Public House |
| Tracks | River and Bridge | Youth Hostel | R Refreshments |
| Footpaths | Sea Embankment | C Camping | PC Toilets |
| | | BK Bunk Barn | P Car park |

**Until reaching point 8 the maps should be read from the bottom working upwards.**

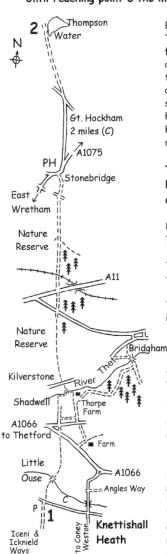

Breckland is the unique region of heathland crossed by Peddars Way. The soil is sandy, dry and infertile, partly due to the Neolithic farming practice of 'slash and burn', crops are prone to drought in a dry summer and much of the area has been planted with conifers by the Forestry Commission. Something of the original character of the area can be seen approaching Thompson Water with Scots pine scattered on open heath. There are several Breckland 'meres' which have higher water levels in summer than in winter! Thompson Water, however, is an artificial lake dug out in the 19$^{th}$ century and more recently has been used for trout farming.

**This section of the route passes through the Stanford battle training area. Do not stray from the path because of the danger from unexploded shells.**

East Wretham Heath, Norfolk Wildlife Trust Reserve: T. 01842 755010.

This section of Peddars Way is at its finest in Spring when the May trees are in bloom.

There is a nature reserve here maintained by the Nature Conservancy in order to preserve some of the traditional Breckland.

Shadwell is named after Chad's well, a shrine for pilgrims. The church tower has been buttressed for over 600 years but still stands strong.

Thetford, meaning 'the people's ford' was the capital of Anglo-Saxon England in King Canute's time. Castle Hill earthworks, 800 year old priory and Ancient House Museum (archaeology) open daily.

Knettishall Heath Country Park preserves some traditional Breckland scenery and is a centre for serious ramblers and gentle strollers. The Angles Way is a 78 mile route to Great Yarmouth, the Icknield Way connects with The Ridgeway and the Iceni Way joins the Norfolk Coastal Path at Hunstanton following an 80 mile Breck and Fenland route around south and west Norfolk. There are also numerous footpaths across the Heath for short rambles.

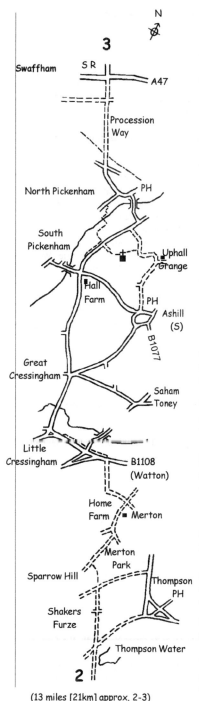

N

**3**

Swaffham    S R

A47

Procession
Way

North Pickenham    PH

South
Pickenham
Uphall
Grange

Hall
Farm    PH

Ashill
(S)

B1077

Great
Cressingham

Saham
Toney

Little
Cressingham    B1108
(Watton)

Home
Farm    Merton

Merton
Park

Sparrow Hill
Thompson
PH

Shakers
Furze

Thompson Water

**2**

(13 miles [21km] approx. 2-3)

Swaffham is an old market town with a lively Saturday market: auctions of bric-a-brac, farm produce, cars and livestock. The village sign recalls the legend of the pedlar of Swaffham. The fine 15th century church has a splendid double hammer-beam roof, with 150 angels carved 500 years ago.

**Access to the Peddars Way from the southeast edge of Swaffham is off the North Pickenham Road by a steep vehicle track eastward, indicated by a metal signpost. Procession Way is reached after one mile along this track**

Procession Way derives its name from the regular religious processions which used it in medieval times.

On the hill towards Uphall Grange is the recently restored St. Mary's Church, Houghton-on-the Hill, where 10th or 11th century wall paintings were found.

South Pickenham Hall to your left is a fine example of a country house built in the neo-Georgian style in 1902 - 05. There is a round tower church nearby.

Great Cressingham is an old village with thatched cottages and a fine 14th century church, with some fine brasses and memories of Cromwell's time.

Watton is an old town with a Norman church and 14th century belfry. Nearby is Wayland Wood or 'wailing wood' - the place of the legend 'Babes in the Wood'.

**North of Home Farm a bridleway leading straight on reaches B1108 on the western edge of Watton, from there a bridleway and road leads to Saham Toney.**

Merton, originally 'mere town', has Roman connections. It has a fine 13th century church.

**On reaching Sparrow Hill go on northwards in the fenced section at the edge of the battle area. This joins a track which enters Merton Park in which you continue due north, finally coming out onto the track which passes Home Farm.**

The village of Thompson existed before the conquest and the church is one the best examples to be found in Norfolk of the early decorated period - 14th century.

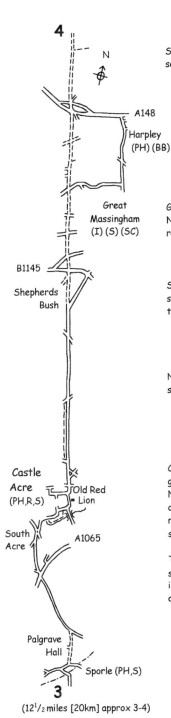

**4**

N

A148

Harpley
(PH) (BB)

Great
Massingham
(I) (S) (SC)

B1145

Shepherds
Bush

Castle
Acre
(PH,R,S)

Old Red
Lion

South
Acre

A1065

Palgrave
Hall

Sporle (PH,S)

**3**

(12¹/₂ miles [20km] approx 3-4)

Several good examples of tumuli - ancient burial mounds - can be seen on this stretch of the route.

Great Massingham is noted for the size of the village pond. Nearby is a fine 14th century church with a pinnacled tower and remains of an 11th century priory.

Shepherds Bush is one of the highest points on the Norfolk stretch of the Peddars Way. Another Roman road, from Brisley to King's Lynn, may have crossed the route about here.

Notice the change in scenery from the infertile Breckland in the south to the highly cultivated rolling hills of west Norfolk.

Castle Acre has Roman, Saxon and Norman connections. The tall gateway opening onto the village green was a gate of the castle in Norman times. The castle hill is on the site of the Roman camp, one of the biggest East Anglian fortresses of the day. A Roman road, from Denver to Smallburgh once crossed west to east just south of the town.

The Norman Priory can be seen from the road by South Acre. It stands next to the river which the monks used to supply fishponds in the priory grounds. The buildings and foundations cover 36 acres. Access is from the street west of the church.

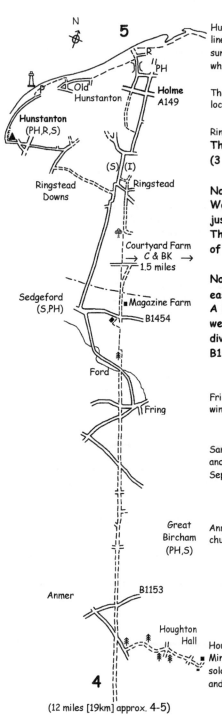

Hunstanton its heyday in the Victorian railway era – the line is now closed. On clear evenings you can watch the sun setting over the sea. The cliffs are striped red and white with carrstone and chalk and Fulmars breed here.

The carrstone is quarried locally and can be seen in many local buildings, although it is not particularly durable.

Ringstead Downs is a chalkland valley, unusual in Norfolk. **This is a quick way into Hunstanton if needed. (3 miles or 5km.)**

**North of the disused railway, follow Peddars Way across the field or use the farm track just to the east - both are rights of way. The Peddars Way continues along the west side of the hedge, up the hill towards Ringstead.**

**North of the Fring to Sedgeford Road, stay east of the hedge until you reach a small wood. A little further on is a sign taking you to the west side of the hedge. Follow signs on a diversion around a field as you approach the B1454.**

Fring has a 14th century church with its belfry windows still intact.

Sandringham (off the route) house, gardens, museum and nature trail. Open Sunday to Thursday, April to September - but closed on special occasions.

Anmer, a village on the Sandringham estate, with a fine church and 16th century Hall.

Houghton Hall built by Sir Robert Walpole, first Prime Minister of England. There is a large collection of model soldiers. Open Easter to September, Sundays, Thursdays and Bank holidays. 2.30 - 5.30 pm. (T. 01485 528569)

(12 miles [19km] approx. 4-5)

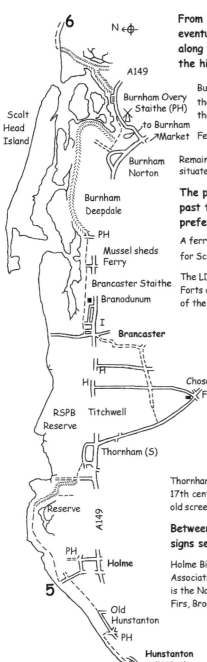

From Burnham Overy Staithe go along the sea bank, eventually reaching the beach. The right of way is along the beach. In May, June and July walk below the high tide line to avoid nesting terns.

Burnham Thorpe (two miles inland) - Nelson's birthplace in the rectory has been demolished. A plaque on a wall marks the place.

Ferry runs from the Staithe to Scolt Head in summer months.

Remains of St. Mary's Carmelite Friary, founded 1241, are situated between Burnham Market and Burnham Overy Town.

The path from the mussel sheds follows the bank top past the houses, you may walk on the marsh if you prefer.

A ferry leaves from Brancaster Staithe in the summer months for Scolt Head National Reserve (tern colonies).

The LDP passes Branodunum the site of one of three Roman Forts on the Norfolk coast. Dalmatian cavalry under "The Count of the Saxon Shore" dealt with invaders from the Continent.

Between Thornham and Brancaster there is no safe route to the seaward side of the A149.

The main road is busy in summer but can not be avoided if visiting the RSPB Reserve. Some roadside footways may help. A quieter route follows a lane one mile inland to reach a footpath going eastwards, and the views are outstanding.

Thornham, formerly famous for its forge, is worth visiting for its 17th century manor house and 14th century church with 500 year old screens.

Between Holme and Thornham observe any diversion signs seen, as the path is subject to erosion.

Holme Bird Observatory is run by the Norfolk Ornithologists' Association and is famous for sightings of migratory birds. Nearby is the Norfolk Wildlife Trust reserve and nature trail. Details: The Firs, Broadwater Road, Holme. Tel: 01485 552240

From Hunstanton go to the lighthouse then along the cliff footpath and behind the le Strange Hotel, turn inland, then after a short way go northeast again along links road, past the club house and skirt south side of golf links to reach Holme via the beach road.

(19 miles [30km] approx. Hunstanton-6)

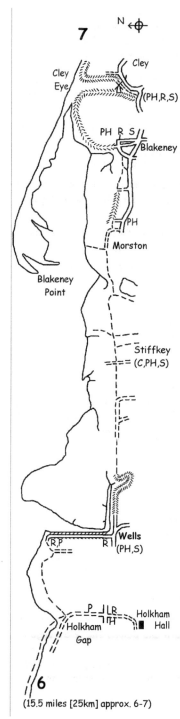

**7**

Cley Eye

Cley

(PH,R,S)

PH R S

Blakeney

PH

Morston

Blakeney Point

Stiffkey

(C,PH,S)

Wells

R,P    R

(PH,S)

P   LR

Holkham

Holkham    Hall

Gap

**6**

(15.5 miles [25km] approx. 6-7)

Glandford Shell Museum (2 miles south from Cley), by the Church - a world-wide collection. Also Tapestry of the Norfolk coast. Open from March to October. Tuesday to Saturday and Bank holidays. 10 - 12.30, 2 - 4.30. GR: 044414.

**From Blakeney, go seawards on the sea wall and cross the River Glaven at the sluice next to A149. Continue to Cley High Street. Turn left along the busy street, but soon turn left to the sea wall and turn right to Cley Mill. Pass to the right of the mill and follow the sea bank to the natural shingle bank at Cley Eye.**

Blakeney used to be a great seaport, provisioning the tall ships used in the crusades. Now the harbour is silted up, the only boats are small pleasure craft and a few passenger ferries making trips to view the seals and land at Blakeney Point in the summer. Ferry also from Morston to Blakeney Point in the summer months.

Saltmarshes are a characteristic of this part of the coast and are a wintering and breeding area for birds. Most of this coast has been purchased by conservation bodies, mainly the National Trust. The plants are specially adapted to withstand occasional inundation by seawater. One of these plants provides the local delicacy "samphire".

Stiffkey famous for its cockles (Stewkey Blues) which are commemorated on the village sign.

**Be careful if you go seawards over the marsh and sandflats. It is easy to lose your way and be cut-off by a rising tide.**

Wells is the only port left on the North Norfolk coast with a usable harbour and until recent years it was occasionally used for the movement of grain and fertilizer, now even that has ceased. A number of fishing and pleasure craft moor here.

Holkham Hall the 18th century home of the Earls of Leicester. (Coke of Norfolk became famous for his Norfolk Rotation and other pioneering agricultural methods). Hall (tapestries and pictures) and Bygones Museum open 1 - 5 pm Sunday - Thursday, June to September and 11.30 - 5pm Sunday and Monday Easter, Spring and Summer Bank holidays. Normally there is all year access to the park walks (fallow deer and bird life).

Holkham pines planted to stop the sand dunes from moving inland, so that the marshes could be reclaimed.

**Go along the beach until you reach the board walk at Holkham Gap, then go inland of the woods and turn east-wards along the track between the woods and the marsh. Go onto the top of the sea bank for the approach to Wells.**

The Cromer Ridge, which is the high ground inland of the town is evidence of glaciation during the ice ages.

Cromer is famous for crab fishing. Sea defences attempt to control the erosion of the cliffs, a problem on this part of the coast. The church tower is the highest in Norfolk after Norwich Cathedral.

Felbrigg Hall a 17th century house with original 18th century furniture. Walled garden, tea shop. National Trust, open April to October. Saturday to Wednesday 1 pm - 5pm

**Leave Sheringham by the sea-front and take the path over Beeston Hump along the cliff. Turn right, following the left edge of a field, over the level crossing and across the main road. Go past Beeston Hall and after a sharp turn left at the bottom of the hill, fork right and go up towards Beacon Hill and Roman Camp. Go over the road and bear left into a footpath in front of a gate. Go down through the wood as far as the Camping Club site, then turn right onto a path, go over Abbs Common and into a green lane. Continue under the railway bridge to reach Cromer.**

Sheringham Park is known for its exotic plants and Rhododendron Woods. Grounds open all the year (NT), there is a fine view of the coast from the Gazebo.

**On the cliff edge route into Sheringham be wary of the cliffs and golfers.** The golfers are not very good at keeping to the fairways

North Norfolk Railway, Sheringham - Weybourne - High Kelling. Steam trains on summer weekends and bank holidays.

'He that would olde Englande win
Should at Weybourne Hope begin.'
(deep water close to the shore would have been of help to an invasion).

Beyond the redundant radar station the sight and sound of old military vehicles comes from the Muckleburgh Collection. Entrance on main road GR: 105428.

**East of Gramborough hill the walking becomes easier.**

**Follow the shingle bank, on top or either side.**
This is remounded mechanically, possibly several times every winter. In February 1996 it was washed over and the salt water flooded the nature reserve. **Mines placed on the beach during the 1939-45 War occasionally reappear, keep a lookout. Bathing is not safe in this area anyway.**

Norfolk Wildlife Trust Information Centre with an exhibition about the North Norfolk Coast is the modern building just east of Cley.

(12 miles [19km] approx. 7- Cromer)

# Weavers Way

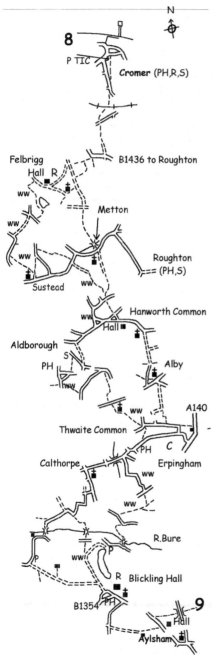

You may now set off on the Weavers Way which is a route developed and published by the Norfolk County Council. It is 56 miles from Cromer to Great Yarmouth. The route was revised in 1997.

The following maps are based on the information in a leaflet, available from: Planning & Transportation, County Hall, Martineau Lane, Norwich, NR1 2DH and local tourist information centres.

**The current route is waymarked with disks on posts, and is shown with "WW" on this map. The previous route is also shown here as it appears on the Explorer Map, published early in 1997.**

Eastern Norfolk has a concentration of round tower churches. There are very few in the country outside Norfolk and Suffolk. W.J. Goode, in his book 'Round Tower Churches of South East England' argues that the construction of many of them is Saxon, dating from as early as 800 AD.

Round tower - St. Peter & St. Paul, Sustead.

St Bartholomew's Church at Hanworth dates from the 14th- 15th century and has fine medieval workmanship.

Round tower – All Saints Church, Thwaite.

Thwaite common, an area of semi-natural grassland which, although privately owned, has rights of pasture over it.

St Margaret's Church, Calthorpe, mainly dates from the 13th century.

Blickling Hall was built 1616-27. One of the most impressive Jacobean houses in England, now owned by the National Trust. The house is open during the season: April to October 1pm – 4.30pm Wednesday to Sunday plus Bank Holiday Mondays. Also Tuesdays in August. Garden as above from 10.30 am. The path around the lake is open at any time.

St. Andrews Church, Blickling, has a number of brasses.

(15 miles [24km] approx. 8—9]

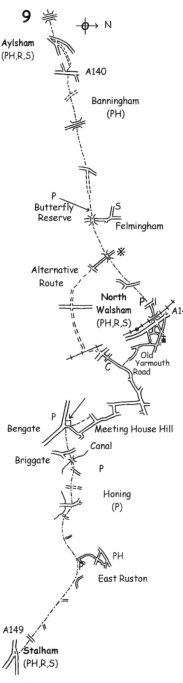

**9**

Aylsham
(PH,R,S)

A140

Banningham
(PH)

P
Butterfly
Reserve
S
Felmingham

Alternative
Route

North
Walsham
(PH,R,S)
A149

Old
Yarmouth
Road
C

P
Bengate
Meeting House Hill

Canal
Briggate
P

Honing
(P)

PH
East Ruston

A149
Stalham
(PH,R,S)

**10**   (14 miles [23km] approx. 9-10)

Aylsham was an important medieval centre for the manufacture of fine linen cloth called Aylsham Webb. It is still a thriving market town.

**Most of the route of this map follows the disused track of the former Midland and Great Northern railway line from King's Lynn to Great Yarmouth. (the sections not following the track are well signposted.**

The line was closed in 1959 and since then a pleasing variety of trees, shrubs and wildflowers have colonised the route making a very attractive path and bridleway.

**Those wishing to avoid North Walsham may use the signposted official diversion to Meeting House Hill.**

This route crosses a battlefield of 1381 during the Peasants Revolt.

North Walsham was another important medieval centre for the weaving industry of the area, with an important market for both wool and finished cloth. Today it is still a market town with considerable industry.

**Go through the town centre past the market cross and leave by the Old Yarmouth Road, follow the footpath and go left into the minor road. At the crossroads turn right into Holgate Lane then go first left, first right, to Meeting House Hill.**

**Turn right to a footpath then left across the field back to the disused railway just before the bypass.**

The village of Worstead, a few miles off the route, from Bengate, gave its name to worstead cloth. This village was extremely wealthy when the wool industry was at its height, as shown by the size of the church. Today it is a small though attractive village.

North Walsham and Dilham Canal was built in the early 19th century to bring coal into North Walsham and goods out, but never a commercial success.

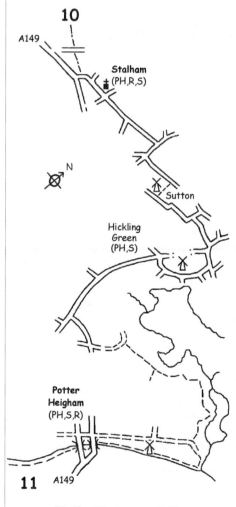

10

A149

Stalham
(PH,R,S)

N

Sutton

Hickling
Green
(PH,S)

Potter
Heigham
(PH,S,R)

11   A149

(10 miles [16km] approx. 10-11)

The final section of The Weavers' Way from Stalham to Great Yarmouth is a further 27 miles (43km).

The route includes extensive Broadland riverside stretches with wide views over open valley land and marshes. There is a striking contrast between the traditional undrained marshland around Hickling Broad and the newly drained agricultural land of the lower Bure and Yare. Many old windpumps formerly used for drainage are notable landmarks.

Stalham, now a holiday centre on the edge of the Broads, has long been a centre for the surrounding countryside: wherries plied between here and Great Yarmouth.

**The Way first follows minor country roads but takes a footpath past Sutton Windmill — the tallest surviving mill in the country with all machinery still in place.**

Hickling Broad national nature reserve covers 1200 acres (485 hectares), including all Hickling Broad and Heigham Sound. Surrounded by reed beds and fen, it is an important habitat for breeding and over-wintering birds. **Please take extra care to protect the wildlife.**

**From the nature reserve entrance to Acle most of the way is along river banks. It skirts the south edge of Hickling Broad and side of Heigham Sound. South of Potter Heigham it follows the Thurne and Bure.**

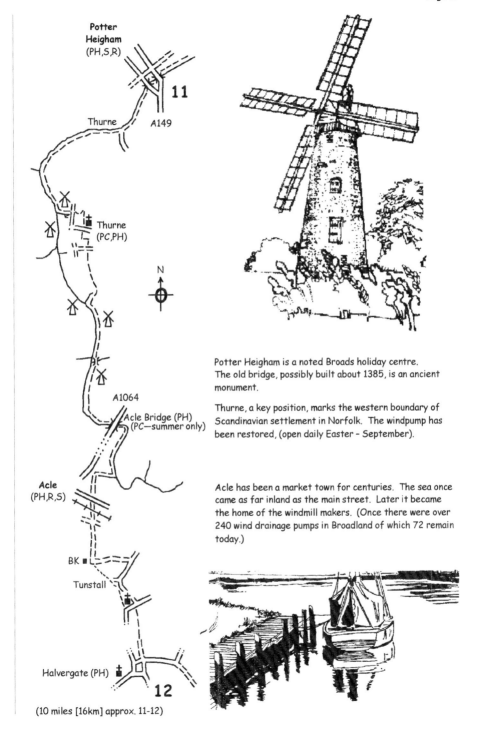

Potter
Heigham
(PH,S,R)

**11**

Thurne    A149

Thurne
(PC,PH)

N

Thurne
(PC,PH)

A1064

Acle Bridge (PH)
(PC—summer only)

Acle
(PH,R,S)

BK ■

Tunstall

Halvergate (PH)

**12**

Potter Heigham is a noted Broads holiday centre. The old bridge, possibly built about 1385, is an ancient monument.

Thurne, a key position, marks the western boundary of Scandinavian settlement in Norfolk. The windpump has been restored, (open daily Easter – September).

Acle has been a market town for centuries. The sea once came as far inland as the main street. Later it became the home of the windmill makers. (Once there were over 240 wind drainage pumps in Broadland of which 72 remain today.)

(10 miles [16km] approx. 11-12)

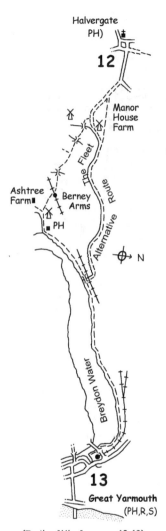

Halvergate
PH)

**12**

Manor
House
Farm

the Fleet

Ashtree
Farm

Berney
Arms

PH

Alternative Route

N

Breydon Water

**13**

Great Yarmouth
(PH,R,S)

(7 miles [11km] approx. 12-13)

The way now crosses low-lying farmland and grazing marshes, some of the largest and most important in the country. Paths often remain boggy till May – boots advised.

The path follows the old marsh road to Manor House Farm, then across the marshes to the Berney Arms to join the path along Breydon Wall and Breydon Sluice. (Please close gates.)

Berney Arms windpump is an ancient monument dating from 1870 (open April—September but times vary).

Breydon Water, a local nature reserve, is important for migrating birds especially waders and wildfowl. Boats raised on stilts are observation huts.

The way follows the flood wall on the north Bank of Breydon Water to Great Yarmouth. Pass Vauxhall Station, continue via North Quay and Market Place to the Tourist Information Centre near Britannia Pier.

Great Yarmouth was built on a sandbar that shifted many times and led to a constant medieval battle to keep the harbour open. The town developed as a fishing port, becoming a popular holiday resort in the 19th century. The old commercial centre faces the harbour and the "new" town of hotels, boarding houses and entertainments faces the sea.

# Transport

**TRAINS** serving the area are run by National Express, East Midland Trains, First Capital Connect. Information on times and fares from staffed stations and National Rail Enquiries: 08457 48 49 50, or visit www.nationalrail.co.uk  These stations may be useful for access to the long distance routes described:

| | |
|---|---|
| Sheringham | Norfolk Coast Path |
| Cromer | Norfolk Coast Path (east) and Weavers Way (north) |
| North Walsham, Acle, Berney Arms, Gt. Yarmouth | Weavers Way |

The nearest railway station for the northern end of the Peddars Way and western end of the Coast Path is King's Lynn. For the southern end of the Peddars Way - Thetford, Diss and Bury St. Edmunds are nearest. Diss is on main London to Norwich line.

**BUSES** - enquiries - Traveline 0871 200 2233 daily, 8.00-20.00. www.traveline.org.uk provides timetables between destinations. Norfolk Green services T.01553 776980, www.norfolkgreen.co.uk  Simonds services T.01379 898202. Mulleys Motorways Ltd. 01284 702830.  Sanders Coaches Ltd. www.sanderscoaches.com First Buses www.firstgroup.com  These routes may be of use:

| | |
|---|---|
| First Eastern Counties **40/41 service** Hourly Sunday more often Monday-Sat. King's Lynn - Hunstanton. | Peddars Way (north) & Norfolk Coast Path (west) |
| Firstbus **X1 service**: Mon-Sat half-hourly, Sun hourly Peterborough - King's Lynn - Swaffham - Norwich | Peddars Way (central - alight at Swaffham). For Weavers Way bus continues to Acle + Gt. Yarmouth |
| Norfolk Green **48 service**  Mon-Sat - 3 times a day King's Lynn - Great Massingham - Harpley | Peddars Way (central near Great Massingham or Harpley) |
| Norfolk Green **36 Coast Bus service**: daily all year, minimum of 5 buses each way, even winter Sundays. Hunstanton - Sheringham | Whole of Norfolk Coast Path could be walked in short lengths over several days using same accommodation for several nights. |
| Norfolk Green Mon-Sat. Sanders Sunday. **29 service** Norwich - Fakenham change here for Wells | Norfolk Coast Path (central) |
| Norfolk Green **X8 service** King's Lynn - Fakenham and **X6 service** Fakenham - Sheringham - Cromer | Links to above service route. Crosses PW near Harpley. Norfolk Coast Path (east) & Weavers Way. |
| Various services from Norwich to: Sheringham, Cromer, Aylsham, Nth.Walsham, Acle, Gt.Yarmouth | Norfolk Coast Path (east) and Weavers Way |
| Simonds **339 & 338 services** - several per day Mon -Sat: Bury St. Edmunds - Garboldisham | Alight at Coney Weston or Barningham. Walk to Knettishall |
| Mulleys **479 service** - Friday only Diss Bus Station to Ixworth, dep 13.30 | Via Hopton, Barningham, Coney Weston. Return bus dep Coney Weston 9.47 Friday |
| Mulleys **425 service** - Monday & Friday only Thetford to Stanton, dep. 12.15 | Coney Weston, Knettishall, Hopton, Barningham. Return bus dep Barningham 9.21 same days. |
| **Flexibus** Watton, Attleborough, Thetford areas. Mon-Fri. 7.30 - 16.00. www.brecks.org.uk | Carries up to 14 people within its area, but must be booked by 17.00 on day **prior** to travel. T.0845 6002315 |
| **Brecks Bus** - operates between Thetford, Brandon and the southern part of Peddars Way. Mon - Fri 9.00 - 16.00    www.brecks.org.uk | Carries up to 5 people anywhere within its area of operation, but must be booked by noon on day **prior** to travel.  T.01638 608080 |

**Note**: Express Bus services between Thetford and Norwich **do not** stop anywhere near the Peddars Way crossing of the A11.

**KNETTISHALL HEATH** is 5 miles (8 kms) by direct road from Thetford railway station, about half being along the busy A1066. **There is no security for cars at Knettishall Heath and they should not be left there except during a day walk.**  There are two 15 mile (24 km) walking routes connecting Knettishall Heath with Thetford using the Iceni Way or with Diss using the Angles Way. (see page 2 for details).

**Baggage Carrying Services.** "Walk Free" will transport your baggage along the Peddars Way or Coast Path. Contact T.01328 711902 or P Way 07787 713459, NC Path 07737 631205 www.walk-free.co.uk for details. Several hotels and B & Bs will also deliver your bags to your next accommodation and some will collect you from the trail, see page 16 and listings for details.

# Accommodation

Although this guide was primarily designed for walkers we recognise that it may be used by riders (both cycle and horse), and some accommodation is included that may be too far away for walkers, so we have indicated distances from the trail – either for the town or village or individual establishments. Within a settlement the listings may be assumed to be close to the centre unless a different distance is indicated. Those on, or within half a mile of the trail are shown with an asterisk (*). Beyond the southern end of the Peddars Way some listings have been included which if they were mid trail could be considered to be too distant, however at the beginning (or the end) of the trail it may be only necessary to cover this extra distance once, and it could prove to be a pleasant addition to the route.

We no longer try to distinguish between guest houses and bed and breakfast, as there now appears to be no significant difference in what they offer, in particular many guest houses no longer offer an evening meal, while a few bed and breakfast proprietors do. It can be assumed that an evening meal will be available at all hotels. We no longer indicate if smoking is allowed, establishments are not now allowed to permit it in public rooms and increasingly they are not allowing it bedrooms either, enquire when booking if this is important to you. We have included some self catering cottages etc., although these, especially in the summer months, may only be available for longer periods than most walkers will require, however if you are making your own transport arrangements, perhaps with two cars, you may find them suitable. Camp sites are assumed to have basic facilities, hot and cold water etc., unless specified otherwise.

Some hotels and B & Bs are willing to pick walkers up from the trail and take them back the next morning and, due to distance, may only be suitable if this service is provided, in which case they are indicated with a hash (#). If you are using a pick-up service we suggest you carry a mobile phone.

The price ranges are based on charges late in 2008 or early 2009, where two, or more, bands are indicated it may be that there are varying facilities in different rooms, or more probably, the charge for singles is significantly more expensive. Prices do change so they should be checked at time of booking

Please let us know of any places that do not meet a reasonable standard or have closed. We should also like to hear of places which are worth including.

Tourist Information Centres listed below provide good coverage of the trails so contact them in case of difficulty finding accommodation. TICs open throughout the year are shown in **bold**.

| **Thetford** | 01842 751975 | Swaffham | 01760 722255 | **King's Lynn** | 01553 763044 |
|---|---|---|---|---|---|
| **Hunstanton** | 01485 532610 | | Wells / Holt /Sheringham / **Cromer** | | 0871 200 3071 |
| Aylsham | 01263 733903 | Potter Heigham | 01692 677016 | **Great Yarmouth** | 01493 846346 |

The following abbreviations have been used:

| | | | | | |
|---|---|---|---|---|---|
| H | Hotel | Std | Telephone area code | £ | to £25 a night |
| I | Inn | GR: | Grid reference | £+ | £25 to £35 |
| PH | Public House | T. | Telephone | £++ | £35 to £50 |
| BB | Bed & Breakfast | F. | Fax | £+++ | Over £50 |
| Y | Hostel - YHA or other | M. | Mobile | D | Double room |
| C | Campsite or possible | EM | Evening meal at B & B | T | Twin room |
| | camping, eg garden of a pub | | (always by advance booking) | F | Family room |
| BK | Bunk Barn | V | Vegetarian menu available | S | Single room |
| SC | Self Catering | P/l | Packed lunches by arrangement | Rstr. | Restaurant |
| B | Bank/Building Society | D/f | Drying facilities | B/m | Bar meals |
| R | Refreshments/Meals | L/f | Laundry facilities | L | Lunch |
| S | Shop (Early closing | Dgs | Dogs by arrangement | E | Evening |
| | Wednesday if not stated) | Cyc | Secure place for cycles | b/a | by arrangement |
| PO | Post Office | Sbl | Stable(s) | Crds | Most cards accepted |
| PC | Toilets | Grz | Grazing | | (or as specified) |
| TIC | Tourist Information | T/p | Tent pitches | Crds/all | All major cards |
| * | On or within .5 mile of trail | C/p | Caravan pitches | | accepted |
| # | Location only suitable if combined with pick up | P/u | Pick up service | } | Charges will vary. **Always** confirm arrangements in advance. |
| | service or similar. | B/d | Onward baggage delivery | | |

Establishments open throughout the year (possibly excluding Xmas and New Year) unless otherwise stated

**Postal towns should not be assumed to have any geographical relevance.**

**Knettishall Heath** Std 01953   For access to Knettishall Heath please see details on previous page.
Car Parking – GR:944807 and GR:956807, but **No Security.**

PC    No Shop. Information Office Open At Weekends. GR:955807

**Coney Weston,** (Bury St. Edmunds) Std 01359   2 miles (4kms) by lane S.E. of Country Park

PH    Peter Kingston, The Swan, Thetford Road, IP31 1DN. GR:955779 T.221295. Food 12.00-15.00
& 19.00-21.00 except Mondays.

**Barningham,** (Bury St. Edmunds) Std 01359   3.5 miles (5.5kms) by minor roads and tracks

BB  SC    College House Farm, Bardwell Road, IP31 1DF. GR:967766. T./F.221512. BB £++ D3 , F1, S1
jackie.brightwell@talk21.com  V. P/l, D/f, Cyc, Dgs, Sbl, Grz,

PH    Royal George, Church Road, IP31 1DD  T.221246  www.royal-george.co.uk  Rstr. & B/m

PO  S    PO, Village Store, 1 Church Road, IP31 1DD

**Bardwell** (Bury St. Edmunds) Std 01359   5.5 miles (8.8 kms) by minor roads and tracks

I    Six Bells Country Inn & Restaurant, The Green, IP31 1AW. GR:946737 T./F.250820
BB £+/£+++ www.sixbellsbardwell.co.uk D7, T2, F1. V, P/l, Dgs, (£10)Cyc (not secure) Crds,

PO    Post Office, Up Street, IP31 1AA

**Garboldisham** (Diss) Std 01953   4.5 miles (7kms) via **Angles Way** (see page 2.)

BB    Ingleneuk Lodge, Hopton Road, IP22 2RQ. GR:002801, T.681541. F.681138. BB £++
www.ingleneuk-lodge.co.uk D2, T2, S1, EM, V, P/l, D/f, L/f, Cyc P/u, B/d Crds

Taxi    Rod Middleton T.681541. rodmid@dsl.pipex.com  Any length of journey. Adv. booking.

SC    Old Mill Farm, Hopton Road, IP22 2RJ  GR:002805     T.681350  www.oldmillfarm.co.uk
D1, T1. D/f, L/f, Cyc, Dgs, (short stays from £175) camping option close to cottage)

PO    PO Stores, The Street, IP22 2QN  T.681217

**Hopton** (Diss) Std 01953   4.5 miles (7.2kms) via **Angles Way** (see page 2.)

BB    The Old Rectory, High Street, IP22 2QX. GR:994790  T.688135, F.681686 BB £++/£+++
www.theoldrectoryhopton.com  D2, T1.  EM, V, P/l, D/f, Dgs £10 per night), Cyc. P/u

PO  S    PO, Norfolk House Stores, Thelnetham Road, IP22 2QY  T.688172

**East Harling** (Norwich) Std 01953. 5 mls (8kms) road, 6 mls (9.5kms) path. Rlwy Stn, Harling Rd. 1.5 mls.

PH  BB    Nags Head, Market Street, NR16 2AD. GR:994863  T.718140 BB £+ D2, T2. V, P/l , D/f, Cyc.
Rstr. & B/m  Tuesday to Sunday  12.00-14.30  18.00-21.30

BB  SC    Dove Cottage, Sue Sturgess, c/o Barn Cottage, Galants Lane, NR16 2NQ  T718628
dssturgess@gmail.com  BB    D2, T1.  V, P/l, D/f, L/f, Dgs, P/u, B/d.    SC min 3 nights

SC    Tapestry Cottage  Mike Dolling 44 White Hart Street,  NR16 1NE  GR:995865  T.718658
F. 717843 www.tapestrycottage.co.uk  D1  L/f, Cyc    min. 3 nights, 7 nights in summer

PH    Swan Inn, Market Street. T.717951, meals,

PO    PO & Card Shop, Market Street, NR16 2AD T.717361

S  R    General Store 7am to 9pm, chemist. Fish & chips (not Sun), Chinese take-away (not Tues)

**# New Buckenham** (Norwich) Std 01953

BB    Pump Court, Church Street, NR16 2BA. T.861039 F.861153 www.pump-court.co.uk  BB £+
D1, T1. F1.  V, P/l, D/f, Cyc, P/u, B/d. Crds

PH    The George, T.860043, meals. The King's Head, T.860487, meals.

PO  S  R    PO, Lovells General Store, Market Place, NR16 2AN.  Fish & chips - Thurs evening, Sat lunch.

**Thetford** Std 01842. 5 miles (8kms) see notes on Transport. TIC

H    Thomas Paine, White Hart Street, IP24 1AA. GR:869833, T.755631. F.766505. BB £+/£++
www.thomaspainehotel.co.uk   D6, T2, F1, S2. V. P/l, D/f, Dgs, Cyc, Rstr. 7 days,  Crds

H    Bell Hotel, King Street, IP24 2AZ. GR:869831 T.754455. F.755552. BB £+/£+++ Crds/all
www.bellhotel-thetford.com D16, T13, S10, F1 & 5 feature rooms. D/f, L/f, Cyc, Dgs, Rstr. & B/m

H    Wereham House Hotel, 24, White Hart Street, IP24 1AD. T.761956.  F.765207. BB £+/£+++
www.werehamhouse.co.uk     D4, T2, S1, F1.  EM, V, P/l, D/f, Cyc, Crds

BB    The Pink Cottage, 43 Magdalen Street, IP24 2PB. GR:873832  T.764564. BB £
mwood.uk@btinternet.com T2.  V, P/l, D/f, L/f, Dgs, Cyc.

**Thetford** Std 01842. 5 miles (8kms) see notes on Transport. (continued)

BB     The Old Rectory, 30 Raymond Street, IP24 2EA. GR:872829 T.765419. BB £
D1, T1, S2. V, Cyc. .

BB     The White House, 4 Raymond Street, IP24 2EA. GR:871829 T.754546. F.890041 BB £
jvmason@btinternet.com D1, T2, S1, F2. D/f, Cyc, P/l (by arrangement), P/u, B/d

PH     Black Horse Inn, GR:873832. Norfolk Plover, GR:865827. Red Lion Inn, GR:872830.

PO     PO, 1 Market Place, IP24 2AA

Taxis     A11 Taxis T.766666, Celebrity Cars T.753232, A1 Cars T.755555, Daleys Taxis T.750777

**West Harling** (Norwich) 2.5 miles (4kms) by footpaths

C     The Dower House Touring Park, East Harling, NR16 2SE. GR:970852. T.717314. F.717843.
www.dowerhouse.co.uk 50 tent pitches £9.50+, 90 caravan pitches £11.50+. Showers, D/f, L/f,
Dgs, Shop, PH. Crds. March – October

**Bridgham** (Norwich) Std 01953 Phone box, no shops.

\* PC Bridgham Heath GR:936871. South side of A11. Car parking. Refreshment stall at times.

**Larling** (Norwich) Std 01953 3.5 miles (5.5km) via A11. 4 miles (6.4km) by minor road

I C     Angel Inn, NR16 2QU. GR:982890 T.717963, F.718561. www.larlingangel.co.uk Restr. B/m
BB £++ D1, T4, V, P/l, Cyc, P/u, B/d Crds/all. 20 tent pitches & 12 caravan pitches, showers.

**East Wretham /Stonebridge** (Thetford) Std 01953.

\* PH     Dog & Partridge, Watton Road, IP24 1QS GR:926907 T.497014.
Phone to check opening hours and whether food is available.

**Great Hockham** (Thetford) Std 01953 2 miles (3 kms)

BB     Manor Farm, Vicarage Road, IP24 1PE GR:951926. www.oaklands4.demon.co.uk/manorfarm
T./F.498204. BB £+ D1, T/F1, S1. V, P/l, D/f, Sbl, Grz, Dgs. Cyc, P/u, B/d. No EM - lift to PH.

SC     Old School Cottage, c/o Richard Levy, Beechwood House Wretham Road, IP24 1NY
GR:952924 T.498277 www.4starcottage.co.uk. D1, T1. P/l, Dgs, D/f, L/f, Cyc

C     Thetford Forest Camping & Caravanning Club Site, Puddledock Farm, IP24 1PA. GR:941925
www.thetfordforestcampsite.com T.498455 150 pitches Caravans. Showers, etc. Dgs. Shop Crds

**Breckles** (Attleborough) Std 01953 3 miles (4.8 kms)

C     Moat Farm Touring Caravan Park & Campsite, Moat Farm, Low Road, NR17 1EP. GR:955941
T.498510, M.07836 784143 www.moatfarm-cp.co.uk showers, Dgs.50p £7.50+ per pitch
15 pitches

**Stow Bedon** (Attleborough) Std. 01953 3 miles (5km)

BB     Home Farm, NR17 1BZ. GR:956962. T.483592. F.488449. www.homefarm-bandb.co.uk
BB £+/£++ D2, T1. V, P/l, D/f, Cyc. P/u, B/d. Sbl, Grz

**Thompson** incl. Peckthorpe (Thetford) Std 01953 1 to 2 miles (1.6 to 3.2 km)

I     The Chequers Inn, Griston Road IP24 1PX. GR:921969. T.483360. F.488092.
www.thompsonchequers.co.uk BB £+/£++ D2, F1. V. P/l, Dgs. Crds.
Rstr. (booking adv.) & B/m Daily 12.00-14.00 18.30-21.15 (Sunday 19.00-21.00)

BB     Mrs. Brenda Mills, Thatched House, Mill Road, IP24 1PH. GR:918967. T.483577.
www.thatchedhouse.co.uk BB £++ D1, T1. V, P/l, D/f, L/f, Dgs, Cyc, P/u, B/d,

BB     College Farm, IP24 1QG. T./F.483318. collegefarm83@amserve.net BB £++
D2, T1. V, P/l, D/f, L/f, Cyc. No EM, lift to PH if raining. Parking while walkers are away

BB     Mrs. Jean Morton, Lands End, Butters Hall Lane, IP24 1QQ. GR:932960 T./F.488070.
jean@jmorton34.freeserve.co.uk BB £+ D3, F1. V, P/l, EM, D/f, Cyc. Sbl, Grz.

PO     PO, Fear Naught, Hall Field Road, IP24 1PT Monday, Tuesday, Thursday & Friday 9.00-13.00

**# Great Ellingham** (Attleborough) Std 01953

BB     Home Cottage Farm, Penhill Rd, NR17 1LS. maureenhcf@waitrose.com GR:002955 T.483734.
BB £+ Serviced apartment (reductions for larger groups or stays of 2 nights or more)
D1, T1, F2. High tea, V, P/l, D/f, Dgs, Sbl, Cyc, P/u.

**# Mundford** (Thetford) Std 01842

BB     Colveston Manor, IP26 5HU. GR:793955 T.878218. F.879218. mail@colveston-manor.co.uk
www.colveston-manor.co.uk BB £+ D2, T1, S1. D/f, P/u

**Merton** (Nr. Watton, Thetford) Std 01953

\* BB C     Terry & Nancy Lordon, Peddars Way B & B, Home Farm, IP25 6QT. GR:900986 T.880180
nancy@lordon.co.uk BB £+ D1. T1 S1. V, D/f, Cyc. B/d Tent pitches

**Griston** (Nr. Watton, Thetford) Std 01953  3 miles (5km)

SC   Mrs. D. Ulrych, Park Farm, Caston Road, IP25 6QD. GR:948989. T.483020 F.483056.
www.parkfarmbreckland.co.uk  D1. Cyc. Min. 3 nights

PH   Waggon & Horses, Caston Rd, IP25 6QD  T.883847  Rstr. B/m 12.00-14.00 18.30-20.30 (21.00w/e)

**Watton** (Thetford) Std 01953  ECD Thursday 1 to 2  miles (1.6 to 3.2 kms)  TIC

H   Hare & Barrel Hotel, 80, Brandon Road, IP25 6LB  GR:906007.  T.882752 F.882312  BB £+/£++
www.hare-and-barrel-hotel-norfolk.co.uk  D6, T6, F2, S4.  V, P/l, Dgs, Cyc. P/u, B/d
Rstr & B/m - L & E 7 days,  Crds.

H   Willow House, 2 High St, IP25 6AE.  GR:916008.  T.881181.  F.885885.  www.thewillowhouse.co.uk
BB £+/£++ D3, T2, F2, S2  V, P/l, D/f, Dgs, Crds.  Rstr & B/m - L 7 days,  E not Sunday.

H   Crown Hotel,  25, High Street, IP25 6AB.  GR:914008.  T.882375.
www.about-norfolk.com/watton/   BB £+/£++   D1, T3, F1  Rstr. & B/m 12.00-14.00 (not E)

BB SC   R Richmond Park Golf Club, Saham Road, IP25 6EA.  GR:908012.  T.881803 www.richmondpark.co.uk
BB £++ Apartments available for BB or SC.  Rstr.

SC   Sandra Coulton, Waylett, 97 Norwich Road, IP25 6DH  GR:923007  sandra@aloz.f2s.com
T./F.884681  D1, L/f, Dgs, Cyc,  sleeps 4, available long or short stays

R   Various cafes, restaurants & take aways (fish & chips, Chinese, etc.)

PO S   PO, 52 High Street, IP25 6AE  T.881201   Tesco Superstore,   Londis early-late,

B   Barclays, NatWest, Lloyds/TSB, Norwich & Peterborough.

**\* Little Cressingham** (Thetford) Std 01953

BB   Jim Wittridge, Sycamore House, IP25 6NE.  GR:873000  T./F.881887.  BB £+
D2, T1, S1.  V, P/l, D/f, L/f, Dgs, Cyc, B/d. No EM, lift to PH.

**Saham Toney** (Nr. Watton, Theford) Std 01953  2 miles (3kms)

H   Broom Hall Country Hotel, Richmond Road, IP25 7EX.  GR:901012.  T.882125.  F.885325.

N 1.8ml 3km   www.broomhallhotel.co.uk BB £++/£+++ D9, T4, F2.  V, P/l, D/f, Dgs, Cyc, Crds.

E 2.5ml 4km   Rstr & B/m - L 7 days, E not Sunday

PH   The Old Bell, Bell Lane, IP25 7HD.  GR:903018.  T.884934.  Rstr.  B/m 12.00-14.00 18.30-21.00

PO S   Post Office & Stores, 24 Richmond Road, IP25 7ER.  GR: 902019.  T.881317

**Great Cressingham** (Thetford) Std 01760   1.5 miles (2.5km)

I   The Windmill Inn, Water End, IP25 6NN  GR:845018.  www.oldewindmillinn.co.uk   T.756232.
F.756400  BB £+/£+++ D6, V, P/l, D/f, Dgs. Cyc, Crds, Rstr. & B/m  5 caravan pitches

BB SC   The Vines, The Street, IP25 6NL.  GR:849016.  www.thevinesbedandbreakfast.co.uk  T.756303
M.07508 195944 BB £/£+  D4, T1, F3, V, P/l, D/f, Dgs, Cyc. Sbl (1 mile away), Grz.  SC cabin

**Ashill** (Thetford) Std 01760  1 to 2 miles (1.4 to 3 km)

C R Spauls Caravan & Camping Park, Brick Kiln Farm, Swaffham Rd, IP25 7BT.  GR:875041.
T.441300.  brick.kiln@onetel.com  18 tent pitches £6.00+ £1 pppn  30 caravan pitches
Showers, etc. L/f, Dgs, Sbl, Grz.  Tea shop nearby

PH   White Hart, Church St. IP25 7AW.  GR: 886043  T.440217 B/m 12.00-14.30(ex Mon) 19.00-21.00

PO   PO, Holmere House, The Green, IP25 7AT  T.441483

**# Bradenham** (Holme Hale) 01760  5 miles

BB SC   The Barn, Ruth Young, Spring Farm, South End, IP25 7QY  GR:917082  www.thenorfolkbarn.com
T.440301  BB £++  V D1 T1  D/f, L/f, Cyc, P/u.  Available as SC or BB

PO   PO, The Lord Nelson, 1 Hale Road, NR25 7RA Tuesday, Thursday & Friday  9.00 -13.00

**\* North Pickenham** (Swaffham) Std 01760

PH C   Blue Lion, Houghton Lane, PE37 8LF.  GR:865069.  T.440289.  mickncaron@btinternet.com
No food.  Backpacker camping in garden, no services.

S   Shop open mornings only . Opposite Blue Lion

**Necton/Swaffham** Std 01760

\* S R   100m, west of route crossing A47: Garage shop & Macdonalds

**Swaffham** Std 01760. 2 mile (3kms) Most things are near the Market Place. TIC

H   George Hotel, Station Street, PE37 7LJ.  T.721238.  www.bw-georgeswaffham.co.uk
BB £++/£+++  D10, T15, S2, F2.  V, P/l, D/f, Dgs, Cyc.  Rstr. all day.

H   Strattons, 4, Ash Close, PE37 7NH.  GR:818091  T.723845.  F.720458.  BB £+++
www.strattonshotel.com.  D5,T1, S5, F5, V, P/l, D/f, L/f, Dgs, Cyc, Crds/All  Restr.

H   Lydney House Hotel, Norwich Road, PE37 7QS.  GR:823088.  T.723355 F. 721410 £++/£+++
www.lydney-house.demon.co.uk  D5, T1, F1, S1.  EM (b/a), V, Crds.

**Swaffham** Std 01760. 2 mile (3km) Most things are near the Market Place. TIC (continued)

| | |
|---|---|
| H | Horse & Groom, 40 Lynn St, PE37 7AX. GR:817091. T.721567. F.725542. Refurbishment 2009 |
| BB | Mrs C.Webster, Purbeck House, 46 Whitsands Road. PE37 7BJ. GR:815090. T.721805. |
| | BB £/£+ D2, T2, S1, F1, EM, V, P/I, D/f, L/f, Cyc. P/u, B/d |
| C | Breckland Meadows Touring Park, Lynn Rd. PE37 7PT GR:809094. www.brecklandmeadows.co.uk |
| | T.721246. £8-£12 p.t.p.n. D/f, L/f, Dgs. Cyc, Showers, Shop, etc. 6 T/p, 35 C/p. over 18s only |
| PH | Greyhound. White Hart, Norfolk Hero. |
| R | Various cafes, restaurants & take aways (fish & chips, Indian, Chinese, etc.) |
| Taxi | 2 & Fro Taxis T.441536 |
| PO | PO, 49-51 Market Place, PE37 7LE T.720277 |
| B | H.S.B.C., NatWest, Lloyds T.S.B., Norwich & Peterborough, Nationwide. |

**Sporle** (Swaffham) Std 01760 0.9mile (1.5 km)

| | |
|---|---|
| BB | Corfield House, The Street, PE32 2EA. GR:849106. T.723636. www.corfieldhouse.co.uk |
| | BB £+ D2, T2. V, P/I, D/f, L/f, Dgs, Cyc, P/u, B/d. |
| BB | Cambridge Cottage. Love Lane, PE32 2EP. GR:844111. T.723718. |
| | BB £ T2. V, P/I, D/f, Dgs, Cyc, B/d, Sbl. Grz . No EM, possible lift to pub. |
| PH | Squirrells Drey, PE32 2DR GR:848113. T.724842. |
| | B/m, Rstr. Fri/Sat 12.00-13.45 Sun 14.00-14.30 Tues-Sat 18.30-21.00 19.00-21.00) |
| S | Threeways Stores, The Street. PE32 2DR GR:849111. T.724300. 6.00 (Sunday 7.30) to 20.00 |
| S | Newsagent & General Store. GR:849113. |

**# Wendling** (Dereham) Std 01362 5.3 miles (8.5 km)

| | |
|---|---|
| H | Greenbanks Country Hotel, Swaffham Road, NR19 2AB. GR:922130 T.687742. Crds |
| | www.greenbankshotel.co.uk BB £++/£+++ D4. T1, F3, D/S1. V, P/I, D/f, Dgs, Cyc, P/u, B/d |
| | Rstr. 12.00-14.30 & 18.00-21.30 |

**# Beeston** (King's Lynn) Std. 01328 7 miles (11 km)

| | |
|---|---|
| BB SC | Holmdene Farm, PE32 2NJ GR:913160 T.701284 www.holmdenefarm.co.uk BB £/£+ D1, T1, S2. |
| | EM, V, P/I, Dgs, D/f. L/f, Cyc, P/u B/d. Sbl, Grz. 2 SC cottages, one sleeps 5, one sleeps 8. |

**# Narborough** (King's Lynn) Std 1760 5.5 miles (9 km) via Nar Valley Way

| | |
|---|---|
| BB | Narborough Trout & Coarse Lakes, Mill View Rooms, Main Rd, PE32 1TE. GR:747132 T.338005 |
| | www.narfish.co.uk BB £+/£++ T3, caravans 20, V, P/I, Cyc, P/u. Crds/all. Min. booking 2 nights |
| SC | Church Farm Holiday Homes, Church Farm, PE32 1TE GR:746130 T.337696 F.337858 |
| | M.07801 641570 www.churchfarmholidayhomes.com 2 cottages - one D1+T1 & one D1. |
| | Dgs, D/f, L/f, Cyc, Sbl, Grz. |
| PO S | PO Stores, Meadow Close, Dennys Walk, PE32 1SZ T.337338 |

**# Castle Acre** (King's Lynn) Std 01760

| | |
|---|---|
| I | Ostrich Inn, Stocks Green, PE32 2AY GR:818152. T.755398. www.ostrichinn.com BB £+/£+++ |
| | D1, T2, S2, F1. V, P/I, , D/f, L/f, Dgs, Cyc, Crds. |
| BB SC | Gill Clarke, Gemini House, Pyes Lane, PE32 2XB. GR:819153 T.755375. BB £ D1, T2, S1 |
| | V, P/I, D/f, L/f, Dgs. Cyc, B/d. Car parking while away. |
| BB SC | Alison Loughlin Old Red Lion, Bailey St. PE32 2AG. GR:818151 T.755557. |
| | www.oldredlion.here2stay.org.uk BB £/£+ D3, T2, F2. V, P/I, D/f, L/f, Dgs, B/d. |
| | Vegetarian wholefood menu only. Hostel type accommodation, group rates negotiable. |
| BB R | Church Gate, Willow Cottage, Stocks Green, PE32 2AE. GR:816150 T.755551. F.755799 |
| | www.churchgatecastleacre.co.uk BB £+/£++ D2, T2. V, P/I, D/f, Cyc, P/u, B/d, Crds. |
| | Tea Room 10.30 - 17.30, closed Monday except Bank Holidays. B & B all year (except Xmas). |
| BB C | Lodge Farm, Rougham Road, PE32 2BS. GR:824170 enquiries@countrysportsonline.com |
| 1.5 miles | T.755506 F.755103. BB £+ D1, T1, F1, EM, V, P/I, D/f, L/f, Dgs, Cyc, P/u. |
| 2.4 km | Sbl, Grz. Possible camping by arrangement. |
| BB | Wicken View, 35 Old Wicken, PE32 2BL GR:804174 T.755652 www.wickenview.co.uk |
| | BB £ D2, V, P/I, D/f, Dgs, Cyc, (1.5 miles north of Castle Acre. 400 metres west of Trail) |
| PH | Albert Victor, Stocks Green. PE32 2AE T.756213. www.albertvictor.net |
| | B/m 12.00-14.00 & 19.00-21.00 V, Beer garden, Dgs |
| R S | Castlegate Stores & Restaurant, Stocks Green. Open 7 Days. |
| S PO | Spar Stores & PO Foxes Meadow, PE32 2AS GR:817154. T.755274. Shop 8.00 to 21.00 7days. |

# East Walton (King's Lynn) Std 01760 5 miles (8 km)

BB  SC  C  Abbey Farm Liveries PE32 1PP  GR:743163  www.abbeyfarmliveries.co.uk  T.337268.

           BB £  D1, T1,  EM, V, P/l, D/f, L/f, Dgs, Cyc, P/u, B/d.

           SC D1, T2    Camping, basic facilities T/p 12 £4+  C/p 6 £4+      Sbl 4 £7, Grz 10 £5

# Gayton 01553 (King's Lynn) Std 01760 5 miles (8 km)

BB      Bridge House, Winch Road, PE32 1QP GR:722191 T.636756 www.bridgehouseholidays.co.uk

           BB £+/£++ D2  EM, V, P/l, D/f, L/f, Cyc, P/u (B1145 crossing GR791211), B/d

**Great Massingham** (King's Lynn) Std 01485 .9 mile (1.5 km)

I        The Dabbling Duck, 11 Abbey Road, PE32 2HN GR:797229 www.thedabblingduck.co.uk

           T.520827 BB £++/£+++ D2, T1. V, D/f, Dgs, P/u, B/d, Crds/all.  Sbl. (locally b/a)

           Rstr. 12.30-14.00 & 18.30-21-00 (except Sunday 12.00-19.00)

SC      Barbara Rogers, 14 Walcups Lane, PE32 2RH GR:796231 T.617558  D1, T1, D/f, L/f, Cyc.

           Short lets sometimes available.

PO S R   Village Store & PO, 12/14 Station Rd, PE32 2HY GR:798229 T.520272 Snacks - take away or

           outside seating area available. Mon-Sat 8.00-13.00, 14.00-17.30 (ECD Wed)  Sun 9.30 - 12.30 .

**Harpley** (King's Lynn) Std 01485    1.8 miles (3 km)

BB      Mrs. Amanda Case, Lower Farm, PE31 6TU. GR:795260. T.520240. BB £+/£++ D2, S1

           V, P/l, D/f, Cyc, Sbl, Dgs (outside)

PH      Rose & Crown, Nethergate Street, PE31 6TW. GR:788258. T.520577. Closed Monday.

           Food 12.00-14.00 Wednesday to Sunday. 18.30-21.00 Tuesday to Saturday 19.00-21.00 Sunday

**West Rudham** (King's Lynn) Std 01485.  3 miles (4.8 km) via A148  3.7 miles (6 km) by path

BB      Oyster House, Lynn Road, PE31 8RW GR:814280 T.528327 www.oysterhouse.co.uk

           BB £+/£++ D2, T1, V, P/l, D/f, Cyc

**Great Bircham** (King's Lynn) Std 01485 1.5 miles (2.4kms)

H        Kings Head Hotel, Lynn Road, PE31 6RJ. GR:767322. T.578265. F.578635 BB £+++ D12,

           www.the-kings-head-bircham.co.uk V, P/l, D/f, L/f, Cyc, P/u by taxi, Crds.  Rstr. L. & E. 7 days.

SC  C    Bircham Windmill, PE31 6SJ. GR:760326.  T.578393 www.birchamwindmill.co.uk . D1, T1 (bunks)

R  S     D/f, L/f, Dgs, Sbl, Grz, Crds/all.  End March-Sept.  T/p 5 basic facilities £10

           Tearoom, Bakery, Mill. Apr-Sept.10.00-17.00

SC      Forester's Lodge, Houghton, PE31 6SU GR:804300  T.528609 www.getley.co.uk D2 T2,

4 miles 6.4 km P/l, Dgs, D/f, L/f, Cyc, P/u, B/d. Sbl.    Minimum stay 3 nights.

S       Country Stores, Lynn Road, PE31 6RJ. T. 578502. Closed Sunday.

PO     Bircham Arts & Crafts, 48 Church Lane, PE31 6XS. T.578203. PO & Gallery.

**Bircham Newton** (King's Lynn) Std 01485 2.2 miles (3.5 km)

SC      Church Farm (Norfolk Disabled Friendly Cottages) Docking Road PE31 6QZ GR:768339.

           T.578603/578354, F.578722 www.norfolkdisabled-friendlycottages.co.uk

           4 cottages  L/f, Dgs, Cyc, P/u, B/d, Sbl, Grz,

**Snettisham** (King's Lynn) Std 01485 3 miles (5 km)

H        The Rose & Crown, Old Church Road, PE31 7LX GR:686343 T. 541382 F.543172

           www.roseandcrownsnettisham.co.uk BB £++/£+++ D6, D/T6, F4 Dgs.

           Rstr. & B/m Mon-Fri 12.00-14.00, 18.30-21.00  Sat/Sun 12.00-14.30, 18.30-21.30

# BB    Twitchers Retreat, 9 Beach Road, PE31 7RA GR:656335   T.543581

5.5miles 9 km www.twitchers-retreat.co.uk  BB £+  T3  EM, V, P/l, D/f, L/f, Cyc, P/u

PO     PO, 11 Alma Road, PE31 7NY  T.541201

**Sedgeford** (Hunstanton) Std 01485    .8 mile (1.3 km)

I        King William IV, Heacham Road, PE36 5LU GR:711366. www.thekingwilliamsedgeford.co.uk

           T.571765. F.571743 BB £++/£++++ D,T, F, S, V, P/l, Dgs, D/f, L/f, Cyc, B/d, Crds Rstr. & B/m.

BB      Park View, PE36 5LU. GR:712365. T.571352. BB £+, D1, T1, S1.

           V, Pl, D/f, L/f, Dgs, Cyc. P/u, B/d.  March – November.

* BB    Magazine Wood, Peddars Way, PE36 5LW GR:722369 T.570422     www.magazinewood.co.uk

           BB £++/£+++ D1, V, P/l, D/f, Dgs, B/d, Cyc.

S       Shop by village green. 7.30 - 18.30.

PO     PO, Village Hall, Jarvie Close, PE36 5NG Tues 13.30-17.30, Thurs 8.30-12.30, Fri/Sat 8.30-10.30

**Docking** (King's Lynn) Std 01485 3 miles (5 km)

BB SC   Holland House PE31 8LH T.518335  www.glavenvalley.co.uk/hollandhouse
           BB £++  D3, T1, V, Cyc, D/f, P/u, B/d     Also cottage SC or BB option

SC     3 Railway Cottages, Station Road, PE31 8LY GR:766377 (contact Steven Ellsey, Home Farm
        Cottage, Main Road, Brancaster Staithe, King's Lynn, PE31 8BJ T.01485 210552)
        www.escape2norfolk.co.uk D1, T1, Dgs, D/f, L/f, 3, 4 or 7 night bookings only

PH    The Railway Inn, Hare Arms, both in Station Road.   King William, High Street

R     Pilgrims Reach, High Street, PE31 8NH T.518383     Fish & chips

PO    PO, Station Road, PE31 8LS T.518755

**\* Ringstead** (Hunstanton) Std 01485

I     Gin Trap, 6 High Street, PE36 5JU GR:706404. T.525264 thegintrap@hotmail.co.uk
       www.gintrapinn.co.uk BB £++/£+++ D3, V, D/f, Dgs, Cyc Crds/all,   Rstr. & B/m

BK C   Courtyard Farm Bunkhouse Barn, PE36 5LQ. GR:729400. T.525251 F.525211. (Lucy Galer)
1.5 miles  courtyardfarm.organic@virgin.net Booking essential. 12 Bunk Beds, (two rooms) £10 per night.
2.5 km    bring bedding and cooking equipment. Dgs, Cyc, Sbl, Grz.  6 tent pitches £5 per night

S     Ringstead Stores, 41 High Street, PE36 5JU GR:707406. T.525270 ECD Tues, Wed, Sat.

**Hunstanton** Std 01485. 3 miles (5kms) via Ringstead Downs & Lodge Farm. **\* Coast Path** Ecd Thursday TIC

BB    The Gables, 28 Austin Street, PE36 6AW. GR:674411 T.532514.  BB £+/£++
       www.thegableshunstanton.co.uk D4, T5, S3, F4.  V, P/l, D/f, Cyc, Crds, B/d.

BB    Mr. & Ms. Sturgess, Garganey House, 46 Northgate. PE36 6DR. T.533269.  BB £/£+
       sturgess@garganey1.fsnet.co.uk D3, T1, S1, EM, V, P/l, D/f, Cyc.

BB    Rosamaly Guest House, 14 Glebe Avenue, PE36 6BS. GR:675413. T.534187.
       www.rosamaly.co.uk BB £+ D2, T1, F1, EM, V, D/f, Dgs. Cyc.

BB    Claremont Guest House, 35 Greevegate, PE36 6AF. GR:675410 T.533171 BB £+ D4, T1, F1, S1,
       claremontgh@tiscali.co.uk V, P/l, D/f, Dgs, Cyc, April to mid November

BB R   Richmond House & Restaurant, 6-8 Westgate, PE36 5AL. GR: 672406. T.532601
       BB £+ D10, T2, S2, EM, V, P/l, Cyc,  Easter to end October

BB    Kiama Cottage Guest House, 23 Austin Road, PE36 6AN GR: 674411 T.533615
       kiamacottage@btopenworld.com BB £+ D2, T2, V, P/l, D/f, Cyc,

BB    Glenberis, 6 St. Edmunds Avenue, PE36 6AY GR:675413 T.533663    £/£+ D2, T1
       www.glenberis.co.uk V, P/l, Dgs, D/f, Cyc, P/u, B/d

BB    Burlington House, 3 Austin Street, PE36 6AJ GR:676411 T.533366 www.burlingtonhouse.info
       BB £+/£++ T1 F2 V, P/l, D/f, L/f, Cyc

BB    Forget me not Guest House, 35 Glebe Avenue, PE36 6BS GR:675413  T.534431
       BB £+ D3, T1, S1, F1. V, P/l, D/f, B/d

Y     Youth Hostel, 15 Avenue Road, PE36 5BW. GR:674406. T.0845 371 9639 F.01485 532632
       www.yha.org.uk hunstanton@yha.org.uk, BB £  9 rooms = 39 beds - 2-8 beds per room EM, V,
       P/l, D/f, L/f, Cyc, Shop, Crds. Closed Sunday & Monday nights.

C     Searles Leisure Resort, South Beach Rd, PE36. GR:671404. T.534211 F.533815 www.searles.co.uk
       289 tent pitches. Showers, laundry, shop, 3 rstrs + fish & chips.

PO B   PO, 21, High Street, PE36 5AB     Barclays, NatWest, Nationwide

S R    Food stores, supermarket. Fish and chips, cafes, restaurants.

**Old Hunstanton** Std 01485  **\* Coast Path**    **PW** 1.3 miles, (2 km) along Coast Path

H     Caley Hall Hotel, Old Hunstanton Road, PE36 6HH, GR: 687423 T.533486. F.533348.
       www.caleyhallhotel.co.uk BB £++/£+++ 40 rooms incl. D/T/S/F. V, P/l, D/f, Dgs. Cyc
       Crds/all Rstr. & B/m, all day, 7 days  closed Xmas one month

H     The Linksway, Golf Course Road, PE36 6JE. GR:688427 T./F.532209
       www.linkswayhotel.com BB £++/£+++ D4 T5 S2 F2 EM, V, P/l, D/f, Crds.

I     The Lodge, Old Hunstanton Road, PE36 6HX GR:684422 T.532896 F.535007
       www.norfolk-hotels.co.uk BB £++/£+++ 16 rooms D/T/S V, P/l, L/f, Dgs, Cyc, Crds.
       Rstr. 12.00-14.00 18.30-21.00

I     Neptune Inn, 85 Old Hunstanton Road. PE36 6HZ. GR:687423 T.532122. F.535314
       www.theneptune.co.uk BB £++£+++ D5, T1. V, P/l, Cyc, P/u, B/d, Crds. Rstr. & B/m L & E

BB    The White Cottage, 19 Wodehouse Road, PE36 6JW. GR:684424 T.532380. BB £/£+,
       D2, T1. EM, V, P/l, D/f, Dgs, Cyc. Parking while walkers are away.

**Old Hunstanton** Std 01485   **\* Coast Path**    **PW** as Hunstanton above + 1.3 miles, (2 km) (continued)

- BB    Lakeside, Waterworks Road, PE36 6JE  GR:687425  T.533763.  www.oldwaterworks.co.uk
BB £+/£++  D4, T2, S1.  V, P/l, Cyc.
- PO S    PO & Driftwood Delicatessen, 38 Old Hunstanton Road, PE36 6HS  T.533197

**\* Holme** (Hunstanton) Std 01485

- BB SC    Mrs Shirley Simeone, Eastgate Cottage, Eastgate Road. PE36 6LL GR:708432 T.525218.
BB £+  T1.  V, P/l, D/f, Cyc.     SC Eastgate Barn sleeps 4
- BB    Mrs. J Reynolds, Meadow View, Manor Court, Eastgate Road, PE36 6LN GR:708432 T.525371.
www.glavenvalley.co.uk/meadowview  BB £+/£++  D2, V, D/f. Cyc, B/d,
secure parking while walkers are away.
- BB    Home Farm Stables, Westgate Street, PE36 6LF. GR:701435    T.525350 or 525610 BB £++
www.homefarmstables-norfolk.co.uk D2,T1, F1.  V, D/f, Dgs, Cyc, Sbl, Grz,
- PH    White Horse, Kirkgate St, PE36 6LH GR:704435. T.525512. Meals 12.00-1400 & 18.00-21.00.

**\* Thornham** (Hunstanton) Std 01485 ECD Thursday

- I    Lifeboat Inn, Ship Lane, PE36 6LT. GR:732435. www.maypolehotels.com/lifeboatinn BB ££+++
T.512236. F.512323 14 rooms D T & F.  V, P/l, D/f, Dgs, Cyc, B/d. Crds. Rstr, & B/m L & E
- I  The Old Coach House, High St. PE36 6LT GR:736433  www.maypolehotels.com/oldcoachhouse
T.512236 F.512323 (reception at Lifeboat Inn) BB £++/£+++ 12 rooms D T & F.  V, P/l, D/f,
Dgs, Cyc, B/d. Crds    Rstr. B/m & Take aways T.512229 Breakfast available for non-residents
- I    The Orange Tree, High St. PE36 6LY. GR:734434. T.512213. F.512424 BB £++ D5, T/F1.
www.theorangetreethornham.co.uk Rstr & B/m V. Dgs.
- BB SC    Mr. & Mrs. M. Wyett, Rushmeadow, Main Road, PE36 6LZ  GR:741434  T./F.512372.
www.rushmeadow.com BB £+/£++  D1, T1,  V, D/f, Cyc,   SC studio (3 day breaks off season)
- PO/S/ R    Post Office , Village Store & Tea Shop, High Street, PE36 6LX T.512194

**Titchwell** (King's Lynn) Std 01485 .8 mile (1.3 km)

- H    Titchwell Manor Hotel, PE31 8BB. GR:760437. T./F.210221. www.titchwellmanor.com
BB £+++  D14, T9, F4.  V, P/l, D/f, L/f, Dgs. Cyc.  Crds/all    Rstr. & B/m
- H    Briarfields, Main Street, PE31 8BB. GR:757437 T.210742. F.210933 www.norfolk-hotels.co.uk
BB £++/£+++  D9, T6, F4.  V, P/l, D/f, L/f, Dgs, Cyc, Crds. Restr. 12.00-14.00 1830-21.00

**\* Brancaster** (King's Lynn) Std 01485

- I    Ship Inn, Main Road, PE31 8AP. GR:772439. T.210333. F.210364    BB £++/£+++  D3, T1,
www.shipinnbrancaster.co.uk  V, P/l, Cyc, B/d, Crds, B/m 12.00 - 14.00 & 18.30 - 21.00
- BB SC    Mrs A Townshend, The Old Bakery, PE31 8AA. GR:775438 (400m. east of Ship) T.210501.
www.glavenvalley.co.uk/bakeryannex BB £+/£++  D/T1,  V, P/l, D/f, L/f, Cyc, B/d
Also available as SC, minimum 3 nights
- BB SC    The Old Stables, Broad Lane, PE31 8AU GR:772439 T.210774.  BB £+/£++  D2, T1
www.burnhamdeepdale.co.uk/oldstables V, P/l, D/f, Dgs. Cyc, B/d. minimum 2 night bookings
weekends May to mid Sept.    SC cottage short lets out of season D1, T1
- S    Shop (community owned) GR:772437 7 days summer 8.00-20.00, winter 8.00-18.00 picnic food
- PO    PO, Main Street, PE31 8BX

**\* Brancaster Staithe** (King's Lynn) Std 01485

- I    The White Horse, PE31 8BY. GR:800442. www.whitehorsebrancaster.co.uk  T.210262
F.210930 BB £+++ D10, T2, S2, , P/l, D/f, Dgs. Cyc, Crds. Rstr. 12.00 - 14.00 & 18.45 - 21.15
- BB SC    Mrs. J. Carrington-Smith, Redwings, Orchard Close, PE31 8BN GR:794441 T.210459.
www.burnhamdeepdale.co.uk/redwings BB £+ T1.  V, P/l, D/f, Cyc, P/u, B/d.  SC (bedsit) T1
- BB    The Smithy, Main Road, PE31 8BJ GR:794443 (opp. Jolly Sailors). T.210638. F.210399
annie.webb@virgin.net BB £+  T1.  V, D/f, Dgs, Cyc,
- PH    Jolly Sailors, PE31 8BJ GR:795444. T.210314. F.210314. www.jollysailors.co.uk Rstr & B/m
12.00 till late - check in low season.
- S    The Stores, Main Road. GR:800444. T.210338.  8.30 to 18.00

**\* Burnham Deepdale** (King's Lynn) Std 01485

- R Y TIC    Deepdale, PE31 8DD. GR:804441 T.210256. F.210158. www.deepdalefarm.co.uk TIC
- Group Y C    Café 07.30-17.00  Deepdale Backpackers. £/£+ D1, T2, £ Quad 1, Dorm 4 (total bunks 28)
V, P/l, D/f, L/f, Cyc. P/u, B/d,  Bedding supplied & equipped kitchen, Crds/all
Deepdale Granary Group Hostel, 18 beds, P/l, D/f, Cyc. Equipped kitchen, bring bedding.
Deepdale Camping, 21 tent pitches, Showers, L/f, D/f, Dgs, Cyc, Grz,

**\* Burnham Deepdale** (King's Lynn) Std 01485 (continued)

S    Deepdale Garage. T.210350 Adjacent to hostels & campsite. Shop 7 days.

**Burnham Market** (King's Lynn) Std 01328 1.5 miles (2.4kms)

H    Hoste Arms, The Green, PE31 8HD GR:831422. T.738777. F.730103. www.hostearms.co.uk
BB £+++ D21, T4, F5, S6. V, P/l, Dgs, Cyc, Crds    Rstr 12.00 - 14.00, 18.00 - 21.00
Annexes - Vine House BB £+++ D7 & The Railway Inn, Creake Road, PE31 8EN BB £++/+++ D6 I
The Jockey, Creake Rd, PE31 8EN. GR:835422. T.738321. www.thejockeyburnhammarket.co.uk
BB £+/£++ D3, T1. V, P/l, D/f, P/u, B/d Crds. Rstr. & B/m, 12.00-14.00(w/e 15.00) 18.00-21.00

BB    Wood Lodge, Herrings Lane, PE31 8DP. GR:830426. T.730152 F.730158 BB £++/£+++
philip.roll@btinternet.com D1, T1, S1 V, Dgs, Cyc, . B/d. 2 nights min. booking at w/ends.

BB SC    The Old Forge, Creake Road, PE31 8EN GR:835420 www.theoldforgeburnhammarket.co.uk
T.730707    BB £+ D2, V, EM, P/l, Cyc, Dgs, B/d discount if arrival on foot or cycle. SC option

BB R    Fishes Café, Seafood Bar & B & B, Market Place, PE31 8HE GR:832422 T.738588 F.730534
www.fishesrestaurant.co.uk BB £++/£+++ D2, Dgs. min 2 nights at w/ends. .
Café Mon-Fri 9.00-19.00, Sat 9.00-20.00, Sun (breakfast) 9.00-11.00

PO    PO, The Green, PE31 8HD

S R    Burnham Market Stores, Humble Pie delicatessen. Lucy's Tea Rooms, various shops

B    NatWest (10.00 - 13.00). Barclays (10.00 - 13.00)

**\* Burnham Overy Staithe** (King's Lynn) Std 01328

BB SC    Mrs. V. Smith, The Brambles, Gong Lane, PE31 8JG.    GR:846437 T.730273. F.730831
burnhambuilder@btinternet.com BB £+ T2. V, P/l, D/f, Cyc, P/u, B/d. SC (optional 1 room)

PH    Hero, Wells Road, PE31 8JE. GR:845443. T.738334. www.theheroburnhamovery.co.uk B/m L/E

**Holkham** (Wells-next-the-Sea) Std 01328 0.5 mile (0.8km)

H    Victoria Hotel, Park Road, NR23 1RG GR:891440.T.711008 F.711009 www.holkham.co.uk/victoria

SC    BB£+++ D8, T1, F1. V, P/l, D/f, Crds. Rstr. T.713230 12.00-14.30, 19.00-21.30
Also 4 SC lodges in Holkham Park.

R    Marsh Larder Tearoom, Ancient House, NR23 1RG. GR:892440.T.711285. July-Sept 10.00-17.00
daily, Nov-June W/end 10.00-17.00, Tues-Fri 10.00.1630 closed Mon (ex Bank hols & half term)

R    Holkham Foods. T.713114. Trailer on car park, Lady Ann's Drive GR:891447. Easter to end Oct.
usually available main holidays weather permitting etc. Good selection hot & cold snacks, drinks.

**\* Wells-next-the-Sea** Std 01328 TIC ECD Thursday

H    Crown, Buttlands, NR23 1EX. GR:916432 T.710209. F.711432. www.thecrownhotelwells.co.uk
BB £++ D8, T2, F2. V. P/l, Dgs, Cyc, Crds/all.    Rstr. & B/m

H    Edinburgh Hotel, Station Rd, NR23 1AE. GR:918435. T.710120. bubynum@hotmail.com
BB £+/£++ D1, T1, S1. V, P/l, Dgs, Rstr. 11.30-14.00 19.00-21.00 (Fri & Sat 18.00-21.00)

BB    Maddie Rainsford, The Old Custom House, East Quay, NR23 1LD. GR:918437 T.711463.
F.710277. www.eastquay.co.uk BB £++/£+++ D2, T1. V, D/f, Dgs, Cyc. Crds.

BB    Mrs J Court, Eastdene, Northfield Lane, NR23 1LH. www.smoothhound.co.uk/hotels/eastdene
GR:919436. T.710381.    BB £+/£++ D2, T1, S1. V, D/f, Dgs, Cyc, B/d.

BB    Kilcoroon, Chancery Lane, The Buttlands, NR23 1ER. GR:917433 .710270. BB £++/£+++ D2, T1.
www.kilcoroon.co.uk EM, V, P/l, D/f, Cyc. P/u, B/d.

BB    Meadowside, Two Furlong Hill, NR23 1HQ GR:914434. .710470 BB £+ D1, T1. V, D/f, Cyc. B/d

BB    Arch House, 50 Mill Road, NR23 1DB GR:912435 T.710112 www.archhouse.co.uk
BB £+/£+++ D9, F1, T2    V. P/l, Cyc, Crds

BB    Manor Farm Guest House, Market Lane, NR23 1HJ GR:916431 T.711392 M.0778 734863
www.manorfarmguesthouse.co.uk. BB £+/£+++ D2, T1, F1. V, P/l, D/f, L/f, Dgs, Cyc, Crds.

BB    Macrimore, Burnt Street, NR23 1HS GR:916431 T.711653 M.07748 365740 BB £++ D1, T2.
www.machrimore.co.uk P/u, Cyc

BB    Shipyard Studio, East Quay, NR23 1LE GR:920438 T.710408    BB £+/£++ D1, D/f, Cyc,

Y SC    Youth Hostel, Church Plain, NR23 1EQ. GR:917433. www.yha.org.uk wellsnorfolk@yha.org.uk
T.0845 371 9544. F./9545 BB£ T2, F6 (31 beds) D/f, L/f, Cyc, Crds, All year.

SC    Hideaway House, Red Lion Yard, NR23 1AX GR:916437 enquiries to Glaven Valley Cottages
T.01263 862133 M.07919653177 www.glavenvalleycottages.com/properties/hideaway_house.html
D2, D/T1, T1(bunk). D/f, L/f, Cyc. short breaks October to March

SC R    The Corner House, Staithe Street, NR23 1AF T.710701, F.710119
chris@cbedford3.orangehome.co.uk D1 (without breakfast £) EM in restaurant, V, Crds

**\* Wells-next-the-Sea** Std 01328  TIC  ECD Thursday  (continued)

    C.    Mill Farm Stables, Mill Road, NR23 1RE  GR:909435  T.710226  15 tent pitches £10+
1.25mile 2km 5 caravan pitches £12+  Dgs, Cyc, showers etc.  Sbl, Grz

  C SC    Pinewoods Holiday Park, Beach Road, NR23 1DR.  GR:914453.  T.710439.  F.711060
  S R    www.pinewoods.co.uk  Showers, L/f, Dgs,  300 T/p (No advance booking for single nights)
    145 caravans  Easter—Decr.  Crds.    SC Lodges & static caravans.
    Café (incl. breakfast) take-aways, General store, 7 days

    I    The Bowling Green Inn, Church Street, NR23 1JB. GR:918432  www.bowling-green-inn.co.uk
    T.710100.  BB available later in 2009    B/m  12.00-14.00 & 18.00-21.00 (Sunday 18.30-21.00)
    I    Globe Inn, The Buttlands, NR23 1EU. GR:916434. T.710206. F.713249  www.holkham.co.uk/globe
    BB £++/£+++ D5, T2.    Rstr. & B/m 12.00 - 14.30, 18.00 - 21.00

  PH R    Pubs, cafes, restaurants and fish and chips along the Quay and Freeman Street
  PO B    Post Office, Station Road, NR23 1AA    Barclays, 1 High Street. T.755500.

**Warham** (Wells-next-the-Sea) Std 01328. 1:3miles (2km)
  PH    Three Horseshoes, The Street, NR23 1NL. GR:948417 . T.710547 Rstr. & B/m,
    www.warham.biz/3horseshoes.  B&B at cottage next door

  BB    The Old Post Office, The Street, NR23 1NL. GR:948417  T.710547 (Three Horseshoes)
    www.warham.biz/old_post_office  BB £+ D3, S1  V, P/l, D/f, Dgs, Cyc.  EM at PH next door.

**Wighton** (Wells-next-the-Sea) Std 01328  3 miles (5 km)
  SC    Nutwood Lodges, Amanda & Jonathan Savory, The Laurels,  NR23 1NX  GR:955397 T.820719
    www.nutwoodlodges.co.uk 3 lodges 1, 2 & 3 bedrooms L/f.

**Stiffkey**  (Wells-next-the-Sea) Std 01328  .6 mile (1 km)
 **\* BB**    Mole Lodge, 84a Wells Road, NR23 1QE  GR:964434  T.830214.
    www.glavenvalley.co.uk/molelodge    BB £+  D1, T1, Dgs, Cyc,
  **\* C**    High Sand Creek, 4 Greenway, NR23 1QF GR:965438. T./F.830235.
    Showers, Dgs.  80 tents. £6.50 - £15.50    April to October.
    I    Stiffkey Red Lion, Wells Road, NR23 1AJ. GR:968433  T.830552.  www.stiffkey.com
    BB £++/£+++  D6, T3, F1,  V, P/l, D/f, Cyc, Dgs, B/d, Crds/all.  Restr. & B/m
  PO S    PO, The Stores, Wells Road, NR23 1QH GR:972442.  Seven days a week.

**Binham** (Fakenham) Std. 01328  4 miles (6.4 km)
  BB    Liz Brown, Abbott Farm, Walsingham Road, NR21 0AW  GR:973389  T./F.830519
    www.abbottfarm.co.uk BB £ + D1, T1, F1  EM, V, P/l, D/f, L/f, Dgs, Cyc, P/u

**\* Morston**  (Holt) Std 01263.
  BB C    Edmund Hamond, Scaldbeck Cottage, Stiffkey Road, NR25 7BJ.  GR:004440  ned@hamond.co.uk
    www.glavenvalley.co.uk/scaldbeck T./F.740188. (daytime T.740144)  BB £+  D1, T1.  V, D/f, Cyc.
    February - November.    6 tent pitches, Shower, £4 per tent + £3 per person per night.
  PH    Anchor Inn, The Street, NR25 7AA  GR:009439.  T.741792.
    Rstr. & B/m, 12.00-14.30, 18.00-21.00 (21.30 Friday/Saturday)  Also afternoon tea.
  R    Willie Weston, van, National Trust car park, www.westonsofblakeney.co.uk  T.741112
    open seal boat times - Summer daily, Winter w/ends only. (See entry under Blakeney below)

**\* Blakeney**  (Holt) Std 01263. Shops and PC at GR:027442.
  H    Blakeney Hotel, The Quay, NR25 7NE. T.740797. F.740795 www.blakeney-hotel.co.uk BB £+++.
    D24, T32, S5,  V, Dgs.  Rstr. & B/m L & E.
  I    White Horse, 4 High Street. NR25 7AL. GR:027441 www.blakeneywhitehorse.co.uk
    T.740574 F.741303. BB £+/£+++ D9. V, P/l,  Cyc, Crds. Rstr. E.  B/m 12.00-14.00 (Sun. 14.30)
  I    King's Arms, Westgate Street, NR25 7NQ  GR:026440. www.blakeneykingsarms.co.uk  T.740341.
    F.740391 BB £+/£++, D4, T2, F1.  V, P/l, , D/f, L/f, Dgs, Cyc.(limited), Crds  Rstr. & B/m, L & E.
  BB    W & R Millard, White Barn, Back Lane, NR25 7NP  GR:031437 (50m from main road)  T.741359
    http://members.lycos.co.uk/raymillard BB £+£++ D1, T1, S1.  V, P/l, D/f, Cyc, P/u, B/d.
  C    Galley Hill Farm Camping, Langham Road, NR25 7PR GR:019428 T.741201
1 mile 1.5km www.glavenvalley.co.uk/galleyhillcamping  Tents & small campervans.  20 t/p. £6 p.p.p.n.
    Showers, no Dgs,  Easter to end October
  S R    Willie Weston's Fish Shop & Sandwich Bar, 5a Westgate Street, NR25 7NQ T.741112
    www.westonsofblakeney.co.uk  Sandwiches, take away meals, tea, coffee.  Summer daily, all day.
    winter, Monday-Friday 9.00-14.00, Saturday all day, Sunday 9.30-16.00

**\* Blakeney** (Holt) Std 01263. Shops and PC at GR:027442. (continued)

    S        Blakeney Delicatessen, 30 High Street, NR25 7AL.  T.740939  F.741710  www.blakeneydeli.co.uk
             Food prepared on the premises, open 7 days 9.00-17.00 in winter - later in summer.

  PO  S    PO, 7-9 Westgate Street, NR25 7NQ        shop 8.00  -  22.00  7 days.

**Wiveton** (Holt) Std 01263 .6 mile (1 km) off LDP at Cley

  I  SC    Bell, Blakeney Road, NR25 7TL. GR:042428. T.740101. M.07974 735474  www.wivetonbell.co.uk
             Rstr. & B/m 12.00-14.15, 18.00-21.15 (not Sun E) Dgs (in bar) BB£++/£+++ D2 (hamper break-
             fast from local baker)    SC cottage D2    2 night min for both BB & SC

  BB  SC    Rosemeade, The Street, NR25 7TH. GR:042432 . T./F.740747    www.stayatrosemeade.co.uk
             BB £+  D1, T1.  V, P/l, D/f, L/f, Dgs, Cyc,    SC chalet D1 T1

  BB  C    Broadview Cottages,  Hall Lane, NR25 7TG GR:040434 www.blakeney-cottages.co.uk  T.740202
             M.07717 167963  3cottages BB £+ October-March D2, S1, F1. V, Cyc, P/u B/d    SC all year

**\* Cley-next-the-Sea** (Holt) Std 01263.

    H        George Hotel, High St. NR25 7RN. GR:045439 T.740652 F.741275 www.thegeorgehotelcley.com
             BB £+/£+++ D11, T1.  V, Dgs.  2 night min w/e    Rstr. & B/m  12.00-14.15 & 18.30-21.00

    I        Three Swallows, Newgate Green, NR25 7TT    GR:047430. T.740526.    BB £+/£++ D4.
             V, P/l, Dgs, Cyc, B/d, Crds/all  B/m 12.00-14.00  & 18.00-21.00  (12.00-21.00 Fri, Sat. Sun)

  BB  SC  R  Cookes of Cley, Coast Road, NR25 7RX  GR:045440  T./F.740776.  www.cookes-of-cley.co.uk
             BB £+/£++  D3, T1, F1.  V, P/l, D/f, Cyc, Crds/all   SC D1 T1
             Bar & Tea Garden 10.00-17.30 summer - daily, winter - week ends only

  BB  SC    Cley Mill, NR25 7RP.  GR:045440  T./F.740209.  www.cleymill.co.uk  BB £++/£+++  D8,
             EM, V, D/f, Dgs, Cyc. Crds/all    SC D2 (can also be let as B&B)

    BB      King's Head Cottage, NR25 7RX  GR:046439  T.740322   www.northnorfolkcoast.co.uk
             richardporter@dialstart.net  BB £+/£++  D1, T1,  V. P/l, D/f, Dgs, Cyc, B/d,

    BB      Rhu-Sila, NR25 7UD  GR:046435  T.740304 www.kbvollmar.de  BB £+/£++  D3, F1, S1, V, D/f.

  S  R     Two shops, takeaway & teashop in High Street.

**Salthouse** (Holt) Std 01263 .5 mile (.8 km)

    BB      Cumfus Bottom, Purdy St. NR25 7XA.  GR:073436  T.741118.  BB £/£+  D2, T1. V, P/l, Dgs, Cyc,

    BB      Springholes, Coast Road, NR25 7XG  GR:079438.  T.740307. www.glavenvalley.co.uk/springholes
             BB £+  D1, V, D/f, L/f, Cyc,

  PH  SC    Dun Cow, NR25 7AJ.  GR 075439.  T.740467. www.theduncow-salthouse.co.uk  Rstr & B/m.
             12.00 - 20.45 (-17.00 Mon/Tues Nov-Feb) Dgs (& muddy boots)  Crds.  SC  2 D/F studio flats
             single night £+ (no 1 night bookings mid season Saturdays)  Basic breakfast pack available.  Dgs

  R  S     Fish & chips      Stores, GR 075439  Closed 17.00  11.00  Eud Wed, Sat & Sun.

**Kelling** (Holt) Std 01263  1 mile (1.6 km)

    H        The Pheasant Hotel, Weybourne Road (A149) NR25 7EG.  GR:098428.  T.588382.  F.588101.
             www.pheasanthotelnorfolk.co.uk  BB £+++  D14, T14, S1.  V, P/l, D/f, Dgs, Cyc, Crds
             Rstr & B/m, L. & E.

    R        The Old Reading Room Gallery, Café.  Closed Mon to Wed Nov to March - otherwise open 7 days

**Kelling Heath** (Holt) Std 01263  1.8 mile (3 km)

  C  SC    Kelling Heath Holiday Park, Sandy Hill Lane, NR25 7HW. GR:109414. T.588181, F.588599
             www.kellingheath.co.uk  showers, D/f, L/f, Dgs, Cyc, Crds  B/m, pizzas, breakfast, EM, V, shop,
             300 t/p  £16.75-£30.50. 36 caravan pitches.  SC 4 lodges & static caravans.  Mid Feb - mid Dec

**Weybourne** (Holt) Std 01263 .6 mile (1 km)

    H        Maltings Hotel, The Street, NR25 7SY. GR:110432.  www.maltingshotel.activehotels.com
             T.588731  BB £++/£+++ D8, T5, F3, S2.  V, P/l, D/f, L/f, Dgs,  Cyc, Crds.  Rstr. & B/m  Closed
             mid December to mid January    5 hook ups

  BB  SC    The Stables, Bolding Way, NR25 7SW  GR:108429 T.588666.  www.boldingway.co.uk
             BB £+/£++ D1, T/F1, EM, D/f, L/f, V, Dgs, Cyc, B/d, Grz. Also self catering cottage D1

    BB      Sheila A Hands, Millpeace, Sheringham Road, NR25 7EY.  GR:115431.  T.588655.  BB £+
             D1, T1. V, P/l, D/f, L/f, Dgs, Cyc.

    BB      Mrs. S R Clarke, Sedgemoor, Sheringham Road, NR25 7EY.  GR:113429.  T.588533.  BB £
             D2, V, D/f. Dgs, Cyc.

    C        Foxhills, NR25 7EH GR:106428  T.588253  £10 per tent for two, plus £1 each addtl. person.
             20 tent pitches.  Showers, limited facilities, no advance bookings

**Weybourne** (Holt) Std 01263 .6 mile (1 km) (continued)

| PH | Ship Hotel, NR25 7SZ. GR:110430. T.588721. Food 11.00 till late (ex 15.00-17.00 Mon-Thurs) |
| S | Spar. GR:110431. Ecd Wednesday and Sunday. Closed 13.00 - 14.00 |

**\* Sheringham** Std 01263 TIC

| H | The Two Lifeboats Hotel, 2 High Street, NR26 8JP. GR:159434 www.twolifeboats.co.uk<br>T.822401. BB £++ D5, T1, F2, S2. V, P/l, D/f, Dgs, Cyc, Crds/all. Meals 12.00-14.30 18.00-21.00 |
| BB | The Melrose, 9 Holway Road, NR26 8HN GR:157428 T.823299. BB £+ D3, T1, S2, F1.<br>www.themelrosesheringham.co.uk V, D/f, Dgs, |
| BB | Claremont B & B, 49 Holway Road, NR26 8HP. GR:156427 T.821889<br>www.claremont-sheringham.co.uk BB £+/£++ D1, T1. V, D/f, Cyc |
| BB<br>.6mile .9km | Holly Cottage, 14a The Rise, NR26 8QB. GR:162426. . www.a2znorfolk.com/hollycottage<br>T./F.822807 BB £+/£++ D1, D/T/F1, V, P/l, D/f, L/f, Cyc, P/u, B/d. Apr-Oct. Min. 3 nights |
| BB | Bayleaf Guest House, 10 St Peter's Rd. NR26 8QY GR:156431 T.823779. F.820041. BB £+/£++<br>www.smoothhound.co.uk/hotels/bayleaf D3, T2, F2. V. B/m 16.00-21.00 |
| BB<br>.6mile .9km | Mrs. Gray, Elmwood, 6, The Rise, NR26 8QA. GR:161426 T.825454. BB £/£+ D1, T1.<br>D/f, Cyc, Dgs, B/d. |
| BB R | Whelk Coppers, Westcliff, NR26 8LD. GR:157434 T.825771. panfoster@hotmail.co.uk BB £+<br>D1, F1. V, P/l, all year. Tearoom June-Octr. + school hols. 7 days 10.00-17.30 (approx.) |
| BB | Camberley House, 62 Cliff Road, NR26 8BJ GR162433 www.camberleyguesthouse.co.uk<br>T.823101 BB £+/£++ V, P/l, D/f, Cyc. |
| BB | Knollside Lodge, 43 Cliff Road, NR26 8BJ T.823320 www.broadland.com/knollsidelodge<br>BB £++ D3, V, P/l |
| Y | Youth Hostel, 1 Cremer's Drift, NR26 8HX. GR:159428. T.0845 371 9040 F.01263 824679<br>www.yha.org.uk sheringham @yha.org.uk BB £ D2, T8, F19, S1. (101 beds). V, EM, P/l,<br>D/f, L/f, Cyc, showers, Crds, Shop February to November |
| R | Several restaurants, cafes and take aways, including fish and chips |
| PO B | PO, 31-33 High Street, NR26 8DS T.710332 Barclays, HSBC, Natwest, Nationwide, etc. |

**Upper Sheringham** (Sheringham) Std 01263 2 miles (3.2 km)

| BB | Mrs. Newstead, Mill Cottage, Pretty Corner, NR26 8TN GR:150410 T.821359<br>www.a2znorfolk.com/millcottage BB £+/£++ D2, T1, V, D/f, Dgs, |

**Beeston Regis** (Sheringham) Std 01263 1 mile (1.6 km)

| BB | Hilltop Outdoor Centre, Old Wood, NR26 8TS. GR:162414 T.824514 F.826137 BB £/£+<br>www.hilltopoutdoorcentre.co.uk D8, T15, F5, V, School holidays only. |

**West Runton** (Cromer) Std 01263

| H | Dormy House Hotel, Cromer Road, NR27 9QA T.837537 www.dormyhouse.net BB £+++<br>D16, F1 Restaurant |
| BB | Mrs. M. Powell, Corner Cottage, Water Lane, NR27 9QP GR:181429 T.838180.<br>BB £ D2, T1. P/l. D/f, Cyc. |
| BB | Mrs K Elliott, Old Barn, Cromer Rd, NR27 9QT T.838285. www.theoldbarnnorfolk.co.uk<br>BB £+/£+++ D2, T1, EM, V, D/f, Dgs. Cyc. |
| BB | Homefield, 48 Cromer Rd, NR27 9AD GR:182427 T.837337. www.homefieldguesthouse.co.uk<br>BB £+/£+++. D4, T2, , V, P/l, Cyc, Crds. Minimum stay 2 nights June - September |
| BB | The Corner House, 2 Station Road, NR27 9QD GR:181427 T.838540<br>www.cornerhousenorfolk.com BB £+/£++ D2, T1 |
| \* C | Beeston Regis Caravan Park, Cromer Road, NR27 9QZ GR:174432. T.823614. F.823944<br>www.beestonregis.co.uk showers, L/f,, shop, Dgs. Crds/all<br>45 tent or caravan pitches £16 - £26. Also 2 fields for group camping. March - October. |
| \* C | Camping & Caravan Club, Holgate Lane, NR27 9NW GR:189419 T.837544.<br>www.campingandcaravanningclub.co.uk Tent pitches flexible Showers, L/f, Dgs, shop.<br>Members £5.25- £5.95 per night. Non-members £6.75 - £7.65 per night |
| PH PO S | The Village Inn, Water Lane, NR27 9QP T.838000 PO & General Store, 40 Cromer Road, |

**Aylmerton** (Norwich) Std 01263

| I<br>.5 mile .8km | Roman Camp Inn, Holt Road, NR11 8QD. GR:184406. T.838291. F.837071<br>www.romancampinn.co.uk BB £++/£+++ D11, T4, F1. V, P/l, Crds. Rstr. & B/m, L & E. garden |
| \* BB | Woodlands G H, Holt Road, NR11 8QA. GR:176408 http://sites.google.com/site/woodlandsgh<br>T.837480 BB £+ D2, T2, S2, F1. V, Cyc. Also 2 SC cottages (one adj., one E. Runton) |

**Aylmerton** (Norwich) Std 01263 (continued)

BB     Eight Acres, Glebe Farm, Holt Road, NR11 8QA   T./F.838094   M.07891 717713
www.theeightacresglebefarm.co.uk £+/£++ D2 V. D/f        5 C/p

BB     Driftway Guest House, The Close, NR11 8PX   GR:180396   T.838589   BB £+/£++   D1, T1   EM

BB     The Eiders, Holt Rd, NR11 8QA T.837280 www.eiders.co.uk   BB £++/£+++   D3 T1 F2. V D/f   Cyc.

**East Runton** (Cromer) Std 01263 .6 mile (1 km)

C     Woodhill Park, Cromer Road, NR27 9PX   GR:194427   T.512242   F.515326   300 tent pitches.
1mile 1.5km www.woodhill-park.com 210 caravans   showers, L/f, Dgs, shop. Crds. March—October.

* C     Manor Farm Caravan & Camping Site, NR27 9PR.   Access from GR:199417.   T.512858.
60 caravan only pitches. 87 serviced tent/caravan pitches, plus unserviced pitches.
Showers, D/f, L/f, Dgs.      www.manorfarmcaravansite.co.uk   ,   April - October.

PH     White Horse, High Street, NR27 9NX. T.519530.   ssmith4857@aol.com   Rstr. & B/m

PH     Fishing Boat, High Street, NR27 9NX.   T.519070   Meals

S     Supermarket, butcher

* **Cromer**   Std 01263 Cabell Road is second on the left east of the rail station. Runton Road runs west
along the front. Third on left is Macdonald Road with several guest houses. TIC

H     Red Lion Hotel, Brooke Street, NR27 9HD.   GR:220423.   T.514964. F.512834   BB £+++.
www.yeolderedlionhotel.co.uk D9, T4, F1, S1 V, P/l, L/f, Crds   Rstr. & B/m 7 days

H     Sandcliff Hotel, 37 Runton Road, NR27 9AS.   GR:213423   T.512888.   F.512785   BB £+/£+++
www.sandcliffhotel.com   D6, T4, S4, F9,   EM, V, P/l, D/f, Dgs, Cyc, Crds

H     Virginia Court Hotel, Cliff Avenue, NR27 0AN   T.512398   F.515529   www.virginiacourt.co.uk
BB £+++   D14, T8, S3.   V

BB     Beachcomber Guest House, 17 Macdonald Road, NR27 9AP T.513398   BB £+   D4, T1,
www.beachcomber-guesthouse.co.uk

BB     Birch House, 34 Cabell Road, NR27 9HX   GR:215421    T.512521   BB £+
www.smoothhound.co.uk/hotels/birchhouse   D3, T2, S1, V, P/l, Dgs, Crds.

BB     Brightside, 19 Macdonald Road, NR27 9AP T.513408   www.brightsidecromer.co.uk BB £+   D3
(min 2 nights) V, P/l

BB     Cambridge House, East Cliff, Tucker Street. NR27 9HD.   GR:220423,   T.512085.
www.cambridgecromer.co.uk   BB £++   D1, S1, T/F4.   V, P/l, D/f, Dgs, Cyc.

BB     Glendale Guest House, 33 Macdonald Road, NR27 9AP. T.513278.   www.glendalecromer.co.uk
BB £/£++   D2, T1, S2.    V, Dgs. Crds March to October

BB     Mrs Rosemary Votier, Morden House, 20 Cliff Avenue, NR27 0AN. GR:221417. T.513396.
www.broadland.com/mordenhouse   BB £+/£++   EM, V, P/l, D3, T2, S1.   EM, V, D/f, Dgs, Cyc,

BB     The Captain's House, 5 the Crescent, NR27 9EX   T.515434   www.captains-house.co.uk   BB £++
D5, EM (winter only) V.

BB     White Cottage, Cliff Drive, NR27 0AW T.512728   www.whitecottagecromer.co.uk   BB £++/£+++
D2, T1. V, P/l, L/f

PO B     PO, 15 Tucker Street, NR27 9HA Barclays, Abbey National, HSBC, Lloyds TSB, Natwest, etc.

Taxis     Ace Cabs T.511749, Country Cars T.515440, My Taxi T.514383

**Roughton** (Norwich) Std 01263 0.5 to 1.5 ( 0.8 to 2.4km) off the LDP.

PH     New Inn, Norwich Road, NR11 8SJ. GR:219368. www.thenewinn-roughton.com T.761389
takeaway     F.768868   Bar meals lunch & evening.   Oriental & British cuisine daily 18.00-22.00 Sunday
Roast 12.00-20.00.   Chinese carry out T.768868   daily 17.00-23.00 except winter Mondays

R     Groveland Fruit Farm, Thorpe Market Road. Café /Restaurant.

PO R     PO, Roughton Service Station, Norwich Road, NR11 8SJ       Fish & chips, eat in or take away

* **Fellbrigg** (Norwich)   Std 01263

R     Fellbrigg Hall (National Trust). GR:193395. T.837444. House open April-Oct except Thurs/ Fri.
Garden open Mar-Oct incl Thurs/Fri during main holiday periods. Refreshments Mar-Oct as
gardens 11.00-17.00. Nov/Dec Thurs-Sun 11.00-16.00.   Jan Sat/Sun 11.00-15.00

* **Aldborough** (Norwich) Std 01263

BB SC     Butterfly Cottage, The Green, NR11 7AA. GR:184343. T.761689/768198. BB £+ D1, F2, S1
www.butterflycottage.com EM, V, P/l, D/f, Cyc, P/u, B/d.   Garden Annexe SC (longer stay)

BB     Aldborough Hall, Hall Road, NR11 7HU. GR:170351   T.570200   www.aldboroughhall.co.uk
2.5 miles 4km BB £++/+++ D3, F1.

**\* Aldborough** (Norwich) Std 01263 1.2 miles (continued)

BB      Calthorpe House NR11 7EU GR:184333 T.761234 www.calthorpehouse.northnorfolk.co.uk
BB £+ D3

PH      The Old Red Lion, The Green, NR11 7AA. T.761451. Meals, 12.00-14.00 19.00-21.00 & tearoom

PH      Black Boys, The Green. NR11 7AA T.768086. Meals

S      Days Stores (Spar), The Green, NR11 7AA. T.761275 8.00-20.00 Mon-Sat. 10.00-18.00 Sun.

PO S      PO Stores, The Green, NR11 7AA T.768198 Butcher, ecd Wednesday, Saturday and Sunday

**Wickmere** Std 01263 1.3 miles (2.1 km)

BB      The Pink House, NR11 7AL GR:173336 T.577678 www.pinkhousebb.co.uk BB £+/£++
D2, T1. P/l, EM (winter only), D/f, P/u, B/d. Possible lift to pub (or cyc. loan)

**Hanworth** Std 01263 1 mile (1.6 km)

C      Deer's Glade Caravan & Camping Park, White Post Road, NR11 7HN GR:215340 T.768633
F.768328 www.deersglade.co.uk tents - main park £4.50/£5.50 pp, Muntjac Meadow August
only £6.50 pp, L/f, D/f, showers, shop, dgs. Free transport to/from local pub.

**\* Erpingham** (Norwich) Std 01263

I      Alby Horse Shoes Inn, Cromer Road (A140), NR11 7QE. GR:207324.
www.albyhorseshoes.co.uk T.761378. BB £+ D2. V, P/l, D/f, Cyc. (P/u & B/d - winter only)
No children under 14. Rstr. (handy for campsite below).

I      Spread Eagle, Eagle Road NR11 7QA. GR:191319. T.761591. www.thespread-eagle.co.uk
Meals - including breakfast. B & B available from March 2009

C      Little Haven, The Street, NR11 7QD GR:203322. www.norfolkguide.co.uk/littlehaven
T./F.768959 25 pitches £11 per tent. March-October. Adults only (16+) Dgs.

R      The Ark The Street NR11 7QB. GR:195322. T.761535. Tues-Sat 12.30-14.00, Sun 19.00-21.30

PO      PO, Alby Service Station, Cromer Road, NR11 7QE

**Calthorpe** (Norwich) Std 01263 1.2 miles (2 km)

I      Saracen's Head, Wolterton, NR11 7LX GR:171323. T.768909. F.769993 BB £++ D5, T1, F1
www.saracenshead-norfolk.co.uk V, P/l, Dgs, Cyc. Rstr & B/m, L. & E.
Bar & restaurant closed all day Monday plus Tuesday lunchtime

**\*Blickling** (Norwich) Std 01263

I      Buckinghamshire Arms, NR11 6NF GR:176286 T.732133 www.bucks-arms.co.uk . BB £++ D3.
V, P/l, Rstr & B/m L. & E.

R      Blickling Hall House & Gardens (National Trust). Park open all year, dawn to dusk.
Garden & Restaurant open Thursday-Sunday all year, Wednesday March to October, Monday
mid July to early September. 10.15-17.15 except Nov-Feb 11.00-16.00 Always closed Tuesday.
House open March to October, days as for garden, 11.00-17.00

**\*Aylsham** Std 01263 Shops. Most things are near the Market Place. TIC

H      Black Boys Hotel, Market Place, NR11 6EH. T.732122. www.blackboyshotel.co.uk Bed £+/£++
(breakfast extra) D4 meals Mon-Sat 12.00-14.00, 18.30-21.00 (21.30 Sat) Sun 12.00-21.00

H      Aylsham Lodge Hotel, 149 Norwich Road, NR11 6JH T.734851 www.aylshamlodge.co.uk
BB £++/£+++ 15 rooms Dgs. Restaurant

BB      Mrs. J Blake, Birchdale, Blickling Road, NR11 6ND. T.734531
www.smoothhound.co.uk/hotels/birchdale BB £+/£++ D2, T1, S1. V, P/l, D/f, Cyc.

BB      The Old Pump House, Holman Rd, NR11 6BY. GR:191269 T.733789. www.theoldpumphouse.com
F.734513 BB £++/£+++ D2, T1, F2. EM, V, P/l, D/f Dgs.

BB      Tim & Janet Bower, Old Mill House, Cawston Road, NR11 6NB (B1145) GR:185266 T.732118.
.7mile 1.2km      timatmill@aol.com BB £+ D1, T1. Cyc.

PH      Feathers, 54 Cawston Rd, NR11 6EB T.732314. Unicorn, 10 Hungate St, NR11 6AA T.732814

R      Full Range - Fish & Chips, Cafes, Restaurants, incl. English, Indian, Chinese

PO B      PO, Hungate Street, NR11 6AA T.733151 Barclays, HSBC, Lloyds TSB, Alliance & Leicester.

**Banningham** (Norwich) Std 01263  1 mile (1.6 km)

PH      Banningham Crown, Colby Road, NR11 7DY.  T.733534.  F.733082.  feneron@msn.com Meals
          Lunch daily 12.00-14.00 (Sun 14.30)    Evening Sun-Fri 19.00-21.00, Sat 18.30-22.00

**\* Felmingham** (North Walsham)  Std 01692

BB      Larks Rise. North Walsham Road, NR28 0JU.  GR:252296 T.403173.
          www.broadland.com/larksrise  BB £ D/F1 (sleeps 4), S1.  EM, V, P/I, D/f, Cyc, P/u, B/d.

S  PO   PO, Felmingham Stores, Nth. Walsham Rd. GR:250293. T.403340.  7.30-17.30, Sun 9.00-16.00

**\* North Walsham** Std 01692. Various Shops

H       Kings Arms, Kings Arms Street, NR28 9JX  T.403054.  F.500095. www.thekingsarmshotel.co.uk
          BB £+/£++  D2, T3, S2. F1, V, P/I, Cyc.  Rstr. & B/m 12.00 - 14.00, 19.00-21.00

H       Beechwood Hotel, 20, Cromer Rd. NR28 0HD.T.403231. F.407284, www.beechwood-hotel.co.uk
          BB £++/+++  D15, T2.  V, P/I, D/f, Dgs, Cyc, P/u, B/d.  Rstr. E (& Sunday L)

H       Scarborough Hill Hotel, Old Yarmouth Road, NR28 9NA GR:291285 T.402151  BB £++/+++
          www.arlingtonhotelgroup.co.uk  8 rooms  B/m & Rstr

BB      Chimneys, 51, Cromer Road, NR28 0HB.  GR:273306.  T.406172.  M.07952 117701
          www.chimneysbb.co.uk BB £+/£++    V, D1, T1, F1.

BB      Green Ridges, 104 Cromer Road, NR28 0HE.  GR:272307 T./F.402448. www.greenridges.com
          BB £+  D1, T1, F1.  EM by arrangement. V, P/I, D/f, Dgs, Cyc, B/d.

BB      Glaven Lodge, 26a, Bacton Road. NR28 9DR. GR:285304.  T.404954. M.07887 601554
          www.glaven-lodge.co.uk BB £+  D1, T1, F1.  P/I, D/f, Dgs (small), Cyc.

BB      The Coach House, Cromer Road, NR28 0HA  T./F.403158  BB £+ D2

BB      Huntersmoon, Field Lane, NR28 9LW  T.404975 e-mail stay-huntersmoon@btinternet.com
          BB £+  D1, EM

BB      Bradfield House, 19 Station Road, NR28 0DZ  T.404352 M.07876 497825
          www.bradfieldhouse.com  BB £+ D3  V

C       Two Mills Touring Park, Yarmouth Rd. NR28 9NA  GR:290287 T./F.405829.  www.twomills.co.uk
          showers, laundry, shop. Dgs. 75 pitches. £14.50-£19.50 per night. 1st March to 3rd Jan. Adults
          only.  Opp. Scarborough Hill Hotel for B/m & Rstr.

PH     White Swan, 12 Church St, NR28 9DA  T./F.402354  B/m 12.00-20.00. Coffee, etc. 11.00-20,00

PH     Bluebell, Bacton Road. NR28 0RA T.404800  Black Swan, Black Swan Loke. NR28 9BX T.402188
          Feathers, Market St. NR28 9DZ T.402630 Orchard Gardens, Mundesley Rd. NR28 DB T.405152

PO  R   PO, New Road, NR28 9AA        English, Chinese, Indian

B       Barclays, HSBC, NatWest, Lloyds TSB, Alliance & Leicester,  Norwich & Peterborough.

**North Walsham** Std 01692  On alternative route ,south of town at crossing of B1150. GR:278283.

BB      The Toll Barn, Heath Road, (Off Norwich Road), NR28 0JB  nola@toll-barn.fsbusiness.co.uk
          T.403638  F.500993  BB £/£+  D1, T1, F1.  (self contained lodges - optional continental break-
          fast £3.50).  Nearest EM at Nth. Walsham, approx 1.5 miles

**Worstead** (North Walsham) Std 01692.  1 mile ( 2km) from Bengate on A149.

BB      The Ollands, Swanns Yard, NR28 9RP.  T./F.535150.  www.ollandsfarm.com BB £+ D2, T1.
          EM, V, P/I, D/f, Dgs, Cyc, P/u, B/d

BB  SC  Churchview House, Westwick Road, NR28 9SD.  GR:301261  T.536863  M.7881 857572
          www.church-view.co.uk  BB £+ D2, T1, F1  5 SC cottages

PH  C   New Inn, Church Plain, NR28 9RW  GR:302260.  T.536296.
          Bar meals 12.00 - 14.00 & 18.30 - 21.00 (not Sunday evening)    20 tent pitches,

PO      PO, Back Street, NR28 9RN  T.536346

**\* East Ruston** (Norwich)  Std 01692.

PH     Butchers Arms, Oak Lane. GR:345282.T.650237 F.651135  B/m Sat 12.00-13.45 & 18.30-21.20
          Sun 12.00-14.00 & 19.00-21.00 Mon-Fri 12.00-14.00 & 18.30-21,30 (21.00 in summer)
          Large groups catered for.  Dgs (in bar)

* **Stalham** (Norwich) Std 01692.

H     Kingfisher Hotel, High Street, NR12 9AN. T.581974. www.kingfisherhotel.co.uk
BB £+++ D5, T1, S2.    V, P/l, D/f, Dgs, Cyc.      Rstr. & B/m 12.00-14.00 & 19.00-21.00

I     Wayford Bridge Inn, NR12 9LL   GR:365243   www.maypolehotels.com/wayfordbridge
T.582414   F.581109   BB £+/£+++   15 rooms   V, Dgs, Crds

PH     Swan Inn, 90 High Street, NR12 9AU.   T.582829.   www.stalhamswan.co.uk   B/m 11.00-21.00

PH     The Grebe, 123 High Street, NR12 9BB   T.580376   B/m

BB     Mary Crucifix, Pear Tree Cottage, High Street, NR12 9AU T.582729   M.07774 909998
BB £/£++ D2, S1, bunk1    D/f, P/u, B/d

BB     Landell, Brick Kiln Lane, Ingham, NR12 9SX.   GR:386256.   T.582349   www.landellbandb.co.uk
.6mile 1km    BB £+/£++   D1, F2.    EM, V, P/l,   D/f, Dgs, Cyc, P/u.

S R     Cottage Bakery, High Street, GR:371252   T.581716   take away sandwiches, pies, etc.

PO B S R   PO, 41 High Street, T.580225   Barclays, NatWest, variety of shops.   Fish & chips take- away

Taxi     Direct Travel T.584877   Stalham Cabs T.581666

* **Stalham Green** (Norwich) Std 01692.

PH BB    The Harnser, The Green, NR12 9QA.   GR:382248. T.580347 F.580401 BB £+   T2, V, Cyc.
Meals L & E.

**Sutton** (Norwich) Std   01692.      .8 mile (1.3km)

H     Sutton Staithe Hotel, NR12 9QS. GR:382237 T.580244. F.583156 www.suttonstaithehotel.co.uk
BB £+/£++ 13 rooms D/T/F/S   V, P/l, Dgs, Cyc.    Rstr. & B/m 12.00-14.00 & 18.00-21.30 7 days

BB     Holly House, The Street, NR12 9RF T.583105 M.07990 633476   clive@furness4438.fsnet.co.uk
BB £+   D1, T1,   D/f, Cyc, P/u, B/d     Min. 2 nights in summer

S     PO GR:385237. Opposite Garden Centre up cul-de-sac. Ecd Wednesday.

* **Hickling** (Norwich)   Std 01692

I     Greyhound Inn & Berties B & B. The Green, NR12 0YA GR:410233   T.598306.   BB £+/£++
www.greyhoundinn.com   D1, T2, S1.   V, P/l,   D/f, Cyc, P/u, B/d.   Rstr & snack bar, L. & E. Dgs

BB     Black Horse Cottage, The Green, NR12 0YA   GR:410233   T./F.598691 BB £+   D2, S1 V, Dgs
www.blackhorsecottage.com

BB     Briarley Lodge, Stubb Road, NR12 0BN   T.598882   www.briarleylodge.fsbusiness.co.uk
BB £/£+ P/l, D/f, Cyc, P/u, B/d

PH     Pleasure Boat, Staithe Road, NR12 0YW.   GR:408225.   T.598211.   Rstr. & B/m

S     Hickling Stores. GR:410235.   Ecd   Wednesday , closed Sunday and 13.00 - 14.00

S     Treasure Box, The Green, NR12 0XN   GR410236 . Newsagent, hot & cold drinks available all day.
Monday-Saturday 7.30-18.30, (except Sat. to 17.30) Sunday 8.00-12.30

**Catfield** (Great Yarmouth) Std 01692 .8 mile (1.3 km)

* BB     The Limes, Limes Road, NR29 5DG   GR:388216   T.581221 www.thelimesatcatfield.com
BB £+/£++ D2, T1.   EM, V

BB     The Old Rectory, School Road NR29 5DA   GR:382212   penny.middleditch@hotmail.co.uk
1.4mile .2km    T.580453   M.7887 584790   BB £++   D2, T1,   Dgs.

PH     The Crown Inn, The Street, NR29 5AZ.    T.580128.   BB   £++   D1, T1.   Meals E

PO     Catfield Stores & PO, The Street, NR29 5AA   T.580262

* **Potter Heigham** (Great Yarmouth) Std   01692.    TIC

I     Falgate Inn, Main Road, NR29 5HZ   GR:414190. T.670003.   BB £   D3,   S1, F1,
V, P/l,   D/f, Cyc, P/u, B/d.    Rstr. & B/m, 12.00-14.30   18.30-21.00   Dgs in bar

BB     Mrs. Molly Playford, Red Roof Farm. Ludham Rd, NR29 5NB   (A1062) T.670604.
1mile 1.6km   gplayford@farming.co.uk BB £    D2, T1.   F1   V, P/l,   D/f, Dgs, Stabling, Cyc, P/u, B/d

C     Causeway Cottage Caravan Park, Tourers & campers. GR:416187   T.670238

PH     Broads Haven Tavern, Bridge Rd. NR29 5JD   T.670329 F.670729   Rstr. & B/m   L & E

PO S R   Post Office Stores, Bridge Rd, GR:414190       Shops, Café, Fish & Chip Rstr. GR:420185.

Page 32

**Bastwick** Repps with Bastwick (Great Yarmouth) Std 01692. .8mile (1.3 km)
BB SC    Grove Farm, Tower Road, NR29 5JN. GR:427177. T.670205 www.grovefarmholidays.co.uk
         BB £+ D1, T1, F1 V       3 SC cottages
\* C      Whitehouse Camping, High Rd, NR29 5JH GR:424180. T.670403. £10-£12
         20-25 tents. Showers. Easter to October.
PO       PO, Repps Village Hall, Mill Road, NR29 5EU Mon & Wed. 9.30-13.30 Tues & Thurs. 9.30-14.00
\* **Repps** Repps with Bastwick (Great Yarmouth) Std 01692.
C        Willowcroft Camping & Caravan Park, Staithe Road, NR29 5JU. GR:414174. T./F.670380.
         www.willowcroft.net 20 tent pitches. Showers £13.50 per night 2 people. All year.
\* **Thurne** (Great Yarmouth) Std 01692
PH       Lion Inn, The Street, NR29 3AP. GR:403158. T.670796. Meals.
**Oby/Clippesby** (Great Yarmouth) Std 01493.
\* C      Bureside Holiday Park, Boundary Farm, Oby, NR29 3BW. GR:403152 T.369233. Showers,
         laundry. 85 tent pitches. £12 per night (2 people) May - September
C SC     Clippesby Hall, NR29 3BL GR:422144 T.367800. F.367809 www.clippesby.com 100 pitches,
1.2mile 2km  £10.50-£25 per night, 2 persons (Easter - end October) showers, L/f, Dgs. 17 SC lodges/
         cottages (all year) Shop, café (inc. breakfast), pub, Rstr. (for residents) (Easter - end Oct)
\* **Acle Bridge** (Norwich) Std 01493
PH       Bridge Inn GR:415116. T./F.750288. www.maypolehotels.com/bridgeinn
         Rstr. & B/m, 12.00-21.00, breakfast (summer only) 8.00-10.00
S        Bridge Stores T.750355
\* **Acle** (Norwich) Std 01493 closest access from Acle Dyke (GR:409107)
H R      Travel Lodge.NR13 3BE. A47/A1064 Roundabout, GR:405104. www.travelodge.co.uk from
         £41.00 for room sleeping 3 adults. 40 rooms. Dgs       Little Chef T.751971
I        Kings Head, The Street, NR13 3DY. T. 750204 F.750713 www.kingsheadinnacle.co.uk
         BB £+/£++ D3, T2, S1. V, P/l, D/f, Dgs, Cyc. Rstr. & B/m L & E.
R        Fern House, The Street, NR13 3QJ T.741000 Coffee Shop, take away, newsagent. 5.00-18.00
R        Grumpys Cottage Restaurant, 23 Old Road T.751111    Cellar Restaurant, The Street, T.751550
         Full River Chinese Takeaway, The Street T.750855
PH R     Hermitage Restaurant & PH. 64 Old Road. NR13 3QP GR:409107. T.750310.
         Rstr & B/m 12.00-14.15, 18.00-21.15. Closed Mondays (except Bank Holidays)
PO B S   PO, 2 Priory Close, T.750201 Barclays, T.634100. Lloyds TSB. T.750325.   Shop GR:402104
Taxi     1st Acle Cars T.750555    Acle Taxi Service T.752222
\* **Halvergate** (Norwich) Std 01493
BB       School Lodge Country Guest House. Marsh Road, NR13 3QB GR:423070 www.uk-guesthouse.com
         T./F.700111.    BB £+/£++ D3, T1 EM, V, P/l, Dgs.
BB       The Manor House, Tunstall Road, NR13 3PS   GR:417089   T./F. 700279
         www.manorhousenorfolk.co.uk D1 T1
BK       Stone Barn. GR:409090. 20 beds. Mrs. More, Manor Farm. NR13 3PS. T.700279. Showers.
         Cooking facilities, (no utensils). Book by phone one day in advance.
PH       Red Lion, Marsh Road. NR13 3QB. GR:424069. T.700317.
\* **Berney Arms** (Great Yarmouth) Std 01493
PH       Berney Arms, NR30 1SB T 700303. Meals. Open April to October.
**Great Yarmouth** Std 01493 TIC
H        Beaumont House Hotel, 52, Wellesley Road, NR30 1EX. T.843957 www.beaumonthousehotel.com
         BB £++/£+++ D6, S1, T1. EM, V, P/l, Cyc.
+        For an extensive list of available accommodation please contact Great Yarmouth Tourist
         Information Centre. T.846345